Hand Lettering for Crafts

D0507152

ROCKPORT

Hand Lettering for Crafts

A Decorative Guide from A to Z

Sandra Salamony

ROCKPORT PUBLISHERS

Copyright ©2001 by Rockport Publishers, Inc.

All rights reserved. No part of this book may be reproduced in any form without written permission of the copyright owners. All images in this book have been reproduced with the knowledge and prior consent of the artists concerned and no responsibility is accepted by producer, publisher, or printer for any infringement of copyright or otherwise, arising from the contents of this publication. Every effort has been made to ensure that credits accurately comply with information supplied.

First published in the United States of America by
Rockport Publishers, Inc.
33 Commercial Street
Gloucester, Massachusetts 01930-5089
Telephone: (978) 282-9590
Facsimile: (978) 283-2742
www.rockpub.com

ISBN 1-56496-741-7
10 9 8 7 6 5 4 3 2 1
Design and layout: Leslie Haimes
Cover design: Leeann Leftwich
Cover Image: Kevin Thomas Photography

Image credit:
   Beardley's Illustrations for Le Morte D'Arthur, Dover Publications, Inc. New York
   KPT Power Photos I

Printed in China.

Contents

Lettering ABCs

Hand lettering, like no other artistic process, can immediately add personality to a craft, whether it's a touch of whimsy, sophistication, or romantic elegance. This book introduces you to many methods of creating personalized hand lettering on your craft projects, including beginning calligraphy with pens and brushes, where each stroke of the pen or brush creates one segment of a letter; decorative painting techniques, consisting of outlining and filling traced letter forms; and specialized crafting processes such as decoupage, chemical rust treatment, and glass etching.

Materials include calligraphy inks, watercolors and gouache, and acrylic and vinyl paints. Craft surfaces are not limited to paper; glazed ceramics and porcelain, glass, metal, fabric, and wood materials are discussed. Specialized transfer processes are introduced, including iron-on color transfer sheets, acrylic gel medium transfers, and even transferring black and white photocopied lettering using wintergreen essential oil.

Many of the hand-lettered crafts available in specialty decorating stores rely on loose, charming printing or handwriting. You may have a hard time accepting your own lettering in that style, and you may feel that perfection never arrives. Always keep an open mind—if you are disappointed in the handmade look of your lettering, don't immediately despair. Sleep on it; tomorrow (or even next week), it will look charming

and personal to you. When adding lettering to a craft, after all the base coating, color washing, and other preparations, it all comes down to one potentially stressful minute—when you begin to apply the lettering and there's no going back. If you feel pressure, take a deep breath, and work on test materials for warm-up practice. Some artists find that it helps to create two projects at the same time, one "for real" and the other as a backup that can become the "for real" project if a mistake is made. Remember, lettering should be fun!

Materials

Basic craft materials

Some basic craft materials are needed for most of the projects, including
- tracing paper
- clean water (preferably distilled) in a jar
- craft knife
- transfer paper and sharp pen, pencil, or stylus for transferring
- straight-edge and a sharp pencil to create guide lines
- a kneaded eraser to remove guide lines and transferred outlines

Media

Colored Pencils and Pastels

These are wonderful for paper applications and can be used with many blending and decorative techniques. A spray fixative is recommended for final artwork, as in memory books or picture frame mats. Watercolor pencils can be washed with water to create varying effects.

Marking Pens

Corresponding to the rise in popularity of scrapbooking, many new pens are being developed with high standards of permanence and acid-free archival quality. Watercolor pens that can be blended with a color wash are popular, as are pens with a brush end to simulate painting. High-precision permanent lining pens are perfect for creating outlines of letters that will be filled later, or for meticulous lettering projects where sharp lines and control are desired. Gel pens write with an opaque colored gel medium that is effective for paper use.

Calligraphy Ink

Calligraphy ink can be used directly from the bottle, or it can be diluted for special effects. It's a very thin medium, so it does not clog calligraphy pen nibs. It is loaded onto a pen nib by dipping or by using a brush or eyedropper to apply ink to the nib reservoir. Calligraphy ink is available in waterproof or nonwaterproof, pigmented or dyed, and in many colors and shades, including iridescent. It can be used with brushes but may damage them over time, so clean your brush carefully and often. For crafts that will be exposed to the sun, permanence of the ink can be an issue; test your ink by writing thick lines on a piece of paper, covering half of the ink with a piece of paper, and taping both papers to a window that receives direct sunlight. After a week, check the inked lines, comparing the covered part to the exposed to see if the ink color has faded.

Watercolor and Gouache

Gouache and watercolors are water-based pigmented media and come in tubes or cake form. They are mixed with water (preferably distilled water to avoid contaminating the paints) to create a smooth paint with many options for textured effects such as dry brushing. Gouache generally has a permanence rating printed on its tube. It is easily used in metal nibs for pen calligraphy and creates a less transparent color in a thicker, creamier form than watercolor. Watercolor's thin texture and transparency allows many decorative options, including blending and color washing. Both clean up quickly and are easy on brushes, though it is always recommended that you promptly clean your brushes after each use.

Acrylic and Fabric Paint

Acrylic paint is a water-based, pigmented medium that provides a highly colored, waterproof coverage when dry. Generally, you should use professional-quality, medium-viscosity liquid acrylics rather than craft acrylic paints; the artist's paints have more pigment than in their crafting cousins, so brushstrokes are less likely to show and coverage is more complete. They are easily mixed to create a wide range of colors, but they are already available in almost any shade you might need. The manufacturers of craft acrylic paints have developed many specialty formulas of paint for special uses, such as painting metal or terra cotta, which are often the best paint for those surfaces. Acrylic paints can damage fine-quality brushes over time, so reserve a set of brushes for acrylic use only, and make sure you clean them promptly after each use. Synthetic brushes hold these paints well and are not as easily ruined as natural-hair brushes.

Fabric paint is an acrylic paint that has been adapted for smooth, permanent coverage on fabric. It often requires heat-setting with an iron or dryer and comes in many forms and colors, including metallic and iridescent finishes. Painting with fabric paint is similar to using other media but may require a firmer brushstroke. For the best results, you might try fixing the fabric to an ironing board or heavy cardboard with fine straight pins to hold it firmly like a canvas.

Oven-Firing Water-Based Enamels

These are a special line of water-based enamel paints that adhere well to glass, glazed ceramics, and porcelain; they are permanent when oven fired at a medium temperature. Make sure to follow the firing instructions on the paint bottle. Surface preparation is important to the permanence of the final letter project—clean the piece well with rubbing alcohol before painting. A wide range of finishes is available, from translucent to opaque, and alternate media can be mixed with the paints to provide a matte or glossy finish. Don't purchase paints that have separated from their medium because they may have lost their ability to bind well to the smooth surfaces of glass and ceramics. It is easy to correct mistakes with these paints; because the dried paint sits cleanly on the surface of the project, you can carefully scrape away small errors with a craft knife, or you can wash away larger areas with water or alcohol before heat setting.

Air-Drying Oil-Based Enamels

These paints provide a thick, opaque coverage on glazed ceramics and glass but are much harder to clean up than water-based enamels. They work well in conjunction with a frisket or adhesive stencil and are durable when dry. Corrections must be made with a solvent such as odorless turpentine, which is also used to clean the brushes.

Other Media

Other media, including milk paint and dry stencil paints; chemical treatments, such as rust-creating chemicals and etching cream; and even plaster are used in the featured projects. Refer to those pages for specific recommendations.

Tools

Calligraphy Pens

Dip pens are the staple of fine calligraphy. You'll want to own broad-edged metal nibs in many sizes to create calligraphic hands such as Foundational, Italic, and Versals, shown in this book. A flexible pointed nib is perfect for the pointed pen lettering illustrated on page 28. Clean and store nibs carefully. For beginning practice, you can use chisel-edged markers, which are available in many sizes and colors—even brush markers for Chinese calligraphy and brush lettering are available.

Calligraphy nibs are available in many shapes, each appropriate to creating a different size or style of calligraphic hand.

Brushes

Whether you use brushes for calligraphy or for trace-and-fill decorative painting, your brushes are the most important tool in your repertoire. A good brush is worth every penny, so buy the best you can afford and take proper care of it. Brush shape is key to good brush performance, so reshape each time you dip a brush in paint. Natural-hair bristles are most appropriate for water-based applications such as watercolors and gouache, but their ability to create a brushstroke without harsh stroke lines will occasionally make them the right tool for acrylic work, too. Acrylic paints can damage natural-hair brushes over time, so be sure to promptly clean and store them. Synthetic-hair brushes, particularly those made specially for decorative painting use, are invaluable for acrylic painting.

Some basic brushes you will find useful are flat- and chisel-edged brushes, a small round brush, and a very small round brush, also called a spotter brush.

Flat Brushes

The flat-edged brush is named for its sharp, tapered chisel edge. Depending on the direction that you use this brush, you can create a thin, controlled hairline or a thick, filled stroke. These brushes can be used successfully with calligraphic alphabets in place of the broad-edged calligraphy pen and are perfect for filling in traced letterforms for decorative painting. Also referred to as chisel brushes, bright brushes, and one-stroke lettering brushes, each type of flat brush has slightly different bristle and handle lengths, resulting in differences in the amount of paint that can be loaded onto the brush and the degree of control necessary to create a steady stroke. Experiment with these brushes to find the one that works the best for you. When buying a flat brush, look for clean, trimmed bristles that taper to a fine edge, with no stray hairs or splits in the bristles.

Round (Pointed) Brushes

Round brushes are versatile tools, as they can create lines from light to heavy depending on pressure and brush direction. Use them to create brush script capitals, as shown on page 22, or for creating loose, painted handwriting. They are also perfect for outlining and filling Versals (page 86), as well as outlining and filling transferred lettering from typefaces for decorative painting. Round brushes are numbered from 000 (very small) to 24 (large). For calligraphic purposes, numbers 1–3 are usually appropriate. For decorative painting, you'll also want to own the very smallest sizes for filling in details and creating decorative accents. When buying pointed brushes, look for those that come to a smooth point, with no stray hairs in sight.

Other Tools

Try using found objects to create stroked lettering in your projects. For example, you could use a broken piece of balsa wood or a stick as a dip pen; even household objects such as cotton swabs and bamboo skewers can be utilized for lettering. Make the most of uneven edges to create unusual and distinctive ink patterns in the lettering.

Various craft surfaces lend themselves to alternate forms of lettering decoration. Use carving tools to incise lettering into soft wood projects and a stylus to carve lettering into soft, malleable materials such as polymer clay.

These coasters are made from polymer clay that was carved with a stylus when soft. The lettering was lightly sanded after baking to remove uneven edges, then emphasized with a burnt umber glaze.

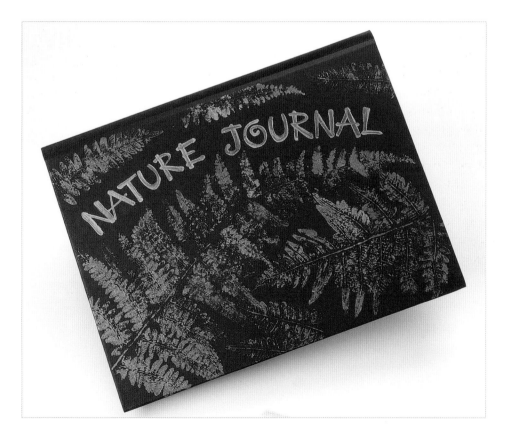

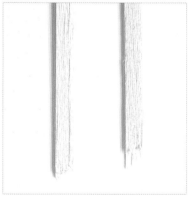

The lettering on Paula Grasdal's nature journal was created with a broken strip of balsa wood and two shades of metallic acrylic paint, enhancing the natural theme of the project.

Time to Begin

Test Your Materials

When working with materials new to you, keep a practice sheet near. As you approach the lettering technique for your craft, do the steps first on the practice sheet. It's much better to learn early that a tea stain or wash should be applied to the surface before the gouache lettering is applied and not after, or else it will all wash away! Testing materials also can result in happy accidents wherein you discover decorative techniques such as watercolor blends or shadow effects on your own.

Beginning Calligraphy

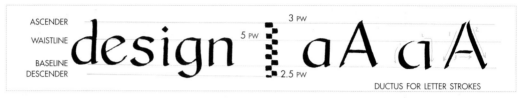

DUCTUS FOR LETTER STROKES

Calligraphy is a wonderful skill for adding decorative lettering to your crafts. To begin, take a look at the Foundational Hand on the facing page. The Foundational Hand was originally developed as a teaching hand, so it is appropriate for beginning study. In calligraphy, letters are created by means of a series of strokes put together in order following a ductus—a series of arrows that show you the direction and order of strokes. The height and placement of the letters follow guidelines such as the baseline, waist, ascender, and descender line. Begin by drawing these lines on a sheet of paper with a sharp pencil and straight-edge.

Letter height is usually measured in numbers of pen widths (pw in the above illustration); for example, a wider nib is used to create larger-sized letters. The stacking rectangles in the example shown above indicate pen widths and letter height. You might want to begin by creating large letters, with a wide nib.

In general, each calligraphic hand utilizes a consistent pen angle, the direction you keep your pen nib in while creating the letters. The Foundational Hand uses a pen angle of about 30°, although this is occasionally changed to 45° on diagonal strokes for a more pleasing appearance.

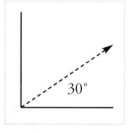

Now it's time to start writing. Make certain that you are sitting in a comfortable position. Dip your pen in the ink to fill the reservoir (or use a brush or eyedropper to place a drop of ink in the reservoir), taking care to not overload the nib. Draw a practice stroke on a piece of scrap paper that you keep nearby—this releases any excess ink you might have in the pen. Warm up by practicing individual strokes from the ductus on facing page. Notice how holding the pen at a consistent angle varies the weight of the strokes you are creating. Now, begin drawing practice letters on your guide rules. You may find it beneficial to practice on tracing paper over a photocopy of the calligraphic exemplars (alphabets), following the ductus (instructional arrows) in order. You'll see the ductus through the tracing paper more clearly if you have access to a light table.

Notice how some letters have small stroked serifs at the beginning and end of strokes. These are created by making a smooth, short motion at the start and finish of the strokes indicated. Both majuscules (uppercase letters) and minuscules (lowercase letters) have these serifs. When you've become comfortable creating letters in Foundational Hand, try the Italic Hand (page 20) and Versals (page 86).

Other calligraphic faces featured in this book are the Italic Hand, Brush Script Capitals, and Versals.

design

DESIGN

DESIGN.

Italic Hand

Brush script capitals

Traditional Versals

abcdefghijkl
mnopqrstuv
wxyz

ABCDEFGHI
JKLMNOPQR
STUVWXYZ
1234567890

Foundational Hand for Crafters ©2000 Mary W. Hart

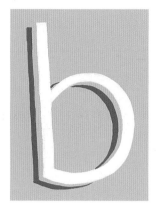

A modern sans-serif letter with a shadow.

A roman letter with a ball terminal, a finial-like cap used with certain roman faces.

letterspacing
letterspacing
letterspacing

"Too loose", "too tight", and "just right" letterspacing.

Movable Type

Letterforms based on the movable type developed for use in printing presses generally fall into two categories: roman (with serifs) and sans-serif. Serifs are the fine lines that finish strokes of letterforms.

The guide rules and terms used for typefaces are slightly different than those used for calligraphic hands, as shown.

These typefaces are useful to crafters for tracing and filling. Above are examples of each kind of typeface in craft use.

Roman
Sans Serif

CAPITAL HEIGHT
X-HEIGHT

design

BASELINE
DESCENDER

Finally, take a good look at letter spacing when tracing outlines. In general, your letter spacing should be close but readable. Like the three bears, the first example is too loose, the second example is too tight, but the third example is just right. It's best to use what is called optical alignment, which means that the spacing looks good to the eye. Pay attention to letters that can be kerned, or tucked in, together, like the n and the g in the above example. That said, however, at times you'll want to extend your letter spacing for special effect or to overlap letters for a playful appearance.

Using Your Own Handwriting

Most of us learned handwriting in school using the Palmer method. Unfortunately, our penmanship usually has degraded since then! You can take control of your handwriting again with new tools: pointed brushes and flexible-tip pointed calligraphy pens.

The two lines at right may be examples of regular handwriting, but they have much more personality when written with a flexible pointed calligraphy pen. See page 28 for more discussion of this tool.

The example at the bottom right shows handwriting with a small round brush. You'll probably need to practice making the strokes wide enough so that they don't fill in, but the result is charming and romantic. See page 30 for more examples.

this is regular handwriting
this is handwriting with emphasis!

Je me suis baigné dans le poème de la mer.

Handwriting with a pointed pen or brush.

Even your printing can be made to look more stylish. By using measured, even strokes with pronounced terminals, your lettering can appear as controlled as an architect's (page 42). And, by ornamenting skeleton letters, you can add a touch of whimsy to ordinary printing (page 26).

Transferred Lettering

The following chapters include many samples of typefaces for tracing and transferring onto your craft surface. Perhaps the easiest way to transfer lettering is with transfer paper, a greaseless paper coated with a colored medium that transfers to many surfaces when pressure is applied with a stylus, a very fine rolling ball pen, or a sharp pencil. It is available in many colors—you'll find that you get the most use from graphite transfer paper, which marks on a wide range of surfaces, including glass and glazed ceramics, and is easy to clean from those surfaces. White transfer paper is also useful for tracing onto dark colors. Never use carbon paper; the residue is not easily removed from many craft surfaces.

Begin by outlining your desired lettering on tracing paper so you can check the letterspacing and size of letters before applying them to your project. Then, place a sheet of transfer paper (coloring side down) between the tracing paper and the craft surface. Outline the letters with a pencil, fine pen, or stylus to trace. You can easily correct major mistakes by cleaning or erasing the traced outlines from the craft surface or by adjusting lines when you paint the final letters. If you use the tracing paper template again on another project, it's beneficial to outline the letters each time with a different color of fine rolling ball pens—that way, you can tell when the outline is completed.

You can make your own transfer paper with tracing paper and a soft pencil. In fact, this method has many benefits when working with paper crafts, as purchased transfer paper can create lines that are thick and unwieldy. To make your own transfer paper, begin as before by tracing your desired letters onto tracing paper. Then, on the back of the tracing paper, rub a soft pencil in the areas where the letter outlines appear. Turn the paper over and retrace the outlines onto your craft surface—the rubbed lead will transfer the lines that you draw.

Another method of transferring lettering is by outlining your tracing paper design with a pounce wheel, creating a series of small holes defining the letters. Tape the template to your decorating surface and pounce with charcoal dust or talcum powder held in a fine-weave rag. The pounced holes appear as dots on your craft surface. This is especially convenient when working with large designs, such as on walls and borders.

Using the Computer

If you have access to a computer, many of the steps to these projects are much easier! It's not cheating to use every tool available to prepare the best possible options for lettering. You can use the computer to print out letters that you'll transfer to project, to plan tricky layouts of text combinations, to help in centering phrases, and to quickly determine the best-sized letters for your project. Don't let the computer make all the decisions for you, however. Look at the output with a careful eye. Are the letters optically spaced the best they can be? Is the leading (space between baselines) too wide or too narrow?

Romantic Lettering

What makes lettering romantic? Often, it is not merely the loops and flourishes of an ornate, decorative script but the elegant, personal touch of handwriting and calligraphy that makes lettering romantic, invoking memories and personality. Adapting your own handwriting by using a flexible-tip pointed calligraphy pen or a round brush is a good beginning to creating romantic lettering, as is adding flourished accents to printing with a marking pen. Learning the calligraphic Italic hand is the starting point for adding measured and even romantic accents to projects with a broad-edged calligraphy pen, and mastering script capitals with a round brush allows you to paint stylish and elegant letters on any surface. Alternatively, creating romantic lettering can be as simple as tracing computer-generated typefaces such as Bickham Script, which imitates the flourishes of old-style roundhand script, and Riva, which adds an element of playfulness to the ornate lettering style. The key to all romantic lettering is to make it look fluid and graceful, composed of smooth and even strokes. Romantic lettering is best suited for projects that are sentimental and personalized—shadow and curio boxes, memory books and travel journals. It is also appropriate for monogrammed projects including napkins, small pillows, greeting cards, and notepaper.

A Simple Italic Hand

Created with a broad-edged calligraphy pen, the Italic hand originated in Italy during the Renaissance. It is a slanted hand that benefits from using the pen at a consistent 45° angle to create smooth and legible strokes. The ductus on the facing page shows the order and direction of penstrokes. It is only a guide; as you learn the letters, you may come up with your own sequence!

abcdefghijklmn
opqrstuvwxyz
ABCDEFGHI
JKLMNOPQ
RSTUVWXYZ
1234567890

© 2000 Mary W. Hart

45°

pen angle

The Italic alphabet consists of slender, slanted letters. Divide the space with rules as shown. Lower case letters stop at the waistline; capitals and ascenders are the same height.

ASCENDER
3 PW
WAISTLINE
5 PW
design
BASELINE
2.5 PW
DESCENDER

aA a A

DUCTUS FOR LETTER STROKES

a b c d e f g h i j k l m n

o p q r s t u v w x y z

A B C D E F G H I

J K L M N O P Q

R S T U V W X Y Z

1 2 3 4 5 6 7 8 9 0

Brush Script Capitals

Created with a round (pointed) brush, Brush Script Capitals are a fluid, elegant presentation of lettering. The pointed brush relies heavily on pressure; the calligrapher changes the position and pressure of the brush to create smooth variations in line weight. Flourishes, which add grace or pizzazz, are best created with a light touch and more speed. Practice these letters, then develop your own style of brush capitals.

A B C D E E

F G H I J J

K L M N O P

Q R S S T U

V W X Y & Z

© Eliza S. Holliday

The angle and pressure of the brush determine the width of the line and weight of the letters. Use the side of the brush for heavier strokes and the tip of the brush for light strokes. Release pressure to create variations in stroke weight, and always use swift, clean, and sure brushstrokes to create these letters.

Bickham Script

Bickham Script is an ornate presentation of romantic lettering influenced by the developments of round-hand script hands in the late eighteenth century and is named after engraving master George Bickham. It is a computer-generated script face, so is presented here for tracing. You can gild, paint, and even etch these letters, perhaps beginning with initials while learning the letterforms, then moving to invitations or other multiletter designs. Be careful, though, not to create a whole word from the capital letters—they are designed for initialing only.

A B C D E F G H

I J K L M N O P Q

R S U V W X Y Z

a b c d e f g h i j k l m

n o p q r s t u v w x y z

1 2 3 4 5 6 7 8 9 0

© Adobe Systems, Incorporated

Riva™

Riva is a computer-generated alphabet that includes a touch of whimsy in its romantic presence. You can trace its lighthearted lines with a pen or use it as inspiration in personalizing your own printing. As with most elaborate script faces, the capitals are designed for initialing purposes only and should be used with restraint.

A B C D E F G H
I J K L M N O P Q
R S U V W X Y Z

a b c d f g h i j k l m
n o p q r s t v w x y z

1 2 3 4 5 6 7 8 9 0

© 1994 International Typeface Corporation

Romantic
Framed Dried Bouquets

T his pretty technique mimicking the thicks and thins of calligraphy with stylized accents is wonderful for inscribing a phrase on crafts or personalizing a memento with a birthdate, name, or special thought. The letters are first drawn as skeleton forms, then made thicker and bolder with careful strokes that add depth and curves, and, finally, made luminous with green and copper accents in iridescent inks. The finished personal, stylized hand-writing follows the curves of the framed dried mini-bouquets, and a splash of iridescence in the ink adds whimsy.

For this project you will need:

3 small bouquets of dried flowers

vintage frame

watercolor paper (use strong room-temperature tea to stain paper before lettering if desired)

permanent archival-quality fine-point pigment liner pen in black

permanent iridescent calligraphy ink in green and copper

small round brush

pencil

kneaded eraser

Lettering Technique

Simple, glowing color added to the counters—the closed area of each letterform—can add delight and charm to words and phrases.

1.

1. This lettering technique adds stylized swirls to personalize simple printing. Before beginning on your final tea-stained paper, practice creating the letters on a scrap piece of watercolor paper. Measure and lightly mark the image area of the frame on the watercolor paper with a pencil. Lightly sketch the baseline and x-height (the height of the lower case letters) curved guide rules that the letters will follow (see page 92 for more guides to placing text on a curve). Draw the skeleton outlines of each letter with a fine-point permanent black liner pen.

2.

2. Embellish the outlines by adding thicker lines, swirls, and curves to stylize the type. Correct any letter curves and proportions that were not sketched correctly in the first step by building up strokes with the pen. You may need to fill in a bit to each curve freehand to preserve the shapely roundness of the letters. Avoid smudges at the phase by working one letter at a time, allowing the ink to dry thoroughly at each application, and being careful to not rest your hand on the inked surface while working.

3.

3. When the letters are as bold as desired, fill in alternating closed areas of letters with iridescent calligraphy ink. Apply the ink with a small round brush, using a scant amount of ink for each letter to avoid blobs and drips. Use short, careful strokes to evenly and accurately spread the ink. If you are using two colors, ink the appropriate spaces in one shade first and let dry before filling in the remaining letters with the other color and a clean brush. When the lettering is finished and completely dry, carefully erase pencil guidelines with a kneaded eraser.

Variation In the initial word, "Le," a playful element is introduced by filling in the closed spaces of the letters. To offset the soft colors of the framed bouquets, light-reflecting copper ink was chosen. For a more formal style, fill in the letterforms with a metallic gold marking pen and use velvet ties to replace the raffia on the bouquets.

Romantic
Calligraphy -Lined Shadow Box

Using a flexible pointed nib with a calligraphy pen can improve your handwriting by emphasizing the contrast between thick and thin strokes. This is the same pen that calligraphers use to create copperplate script, but before studying that calligraphic hand, try using the pen with your own handwriting—you'll be surprised at the artistic effects you can create. You can use the finished lettering to line a shadowbox collage, as shown here, perhaps photocopying the final lettering onto different papers for variation. You can use this writing technique for invitations, memory books, picture mats, and recipe collections as well.

For this project you will need:

- shadow box, finished as desired
- pointed flexible pen nib
- calligraphy pen holder
- black calligraphy ink
- gum arabic (optional)
- cream laid paper or other smooth finished paper
- pencil and straight-edge
- painted wooden egg and other found objects as desired to fill the shadow box

Lettering Technique

By using a flexible pointed calligraphy pen with ink, you can adapt your regular handwriting into an elegant and distinctive cursive with pronounced contrast between thick and thin strokes.

this is regular handwriting

this is handwriting with emphasis!

1.

birds, of all wild creatures, generat
most interest because of the large
number of colorful species, their cr
songs, and especially their long se
annual migrations that bring the
of the unexpected to the alert wat

Birds, of all species of wild cre
generate by far the most inte.
because of the large numbers of c
species, their variations in smé

2.

Flourishes are Nice as Well

3.

1. Lightly draw baseline and waistline guides on your writing paper with a pencil and straight-edge. Dip your pen in the ink (being careful not to overload) and begin writing, refilling the pen as necessary. Hold the pen in the same direction as your letter strokes; if you want your handwriting to be strongly slanted to the right, angle your paper so that the lettering will be slanted when the paper is turned straight. Use varying pressure on the pen to create strokes: heavy pressure on downstrokes for thick lines and light pressure on upstrokes for hairlines or flourishes. Adding gum arabic to your ink makes it more viscous and easy to use. A recommended formula is twenty-five drops per bottle of ink.

2. Unlike calligraphy with a broad-edged pen nib, where the pen is lifted from the paper to make each stroke, the pointed pen allows you to write naturally in a smooth flowing motion. Practice making connecting cursive letters s and e to become familiar with the variations in pressure needed to utilize this pen. Experiment with different writing styles. When you find a style you like, complete a page, then photocopy it for use in your project.

3. When you become more adept at using the pointed pen, experiment with adding flourishes for a grander style.

 Variation Add a subtle dreamlike quality to your writing by using two shades of calligraphy ink and water. Apply two related colors of ink to your pen nib with an eyedropper or brush, alternating colors as desired. Or, alternate the ink with a drop of water—the writing will gradually become lighter as you use the pen.

Birds, of all species of wild
creatures generate by far
the most interest because of
the large numbers of colorful
species

Romantic
Seaside Curio Box

Filled with memories of seaside vacations, this curio box would be romantic without any lettering at all, so adapting your own handwriting into a subtle wash of charming, loopy script letterforms is the perfect addition. You'll be surprised how quickly your can relearn handwriting while working with a brush and ink, making your letters wider and more ornate. Use this writing to add sentimental and meaningful phrases on picture frames, collage greeting cards, or any other personalized project.

For this project you will need:

unfinished wooden square memory box with four openings

desired stains and pigments to finish

sepia calligraphy ink

small round brush

bronze gel pen

Lettering Technique

Your own handwriting can be adapted with the pointed round brush, resulting in charming, romantic lettering.

Je me suis baigné

1.

Je me suis

le poème

2.

Je me suis baigné dans
le poème de la mer.

3.

1. Take a look at your own handwriting when using a fine pen. Most people become tense and impatient when writing, so handwriting is often narrow and cramped. Printed letters are often substituted for traditional cursive letters, loops become tight, and i's are not dotted.

2. Try writing the same phrase with a small round brush and sepia calligraphy ink on scrap paper. Take a deep breath to relax before beginning. Make the loops of the e's and l's wide and loose so the ink doesn't fill in the letters. Extend curves wherever possible, such as on the capital J, the lowercase s, and the lowercase p. Experiment with brush position and brush angle—get a fine line with little pressure, a thicker line with more pressure. Then apply the writing to the outside of your finished box. Depending on the stain, color wash, or wax used to finish the box, the sepia ink may soak in to the wood. Emphasize this dreamy appearance by lightly sanding the lettering, allowing the finish to show through.

3. To enhance the visibility of the letters, outline them with a bronze gel pen, following the lines of the letters with loose and clean strokes. Repeat the technique on the other side of the box, perhaps using the translation of the quotation.

ABCD Variation Imitating French avant-garde artists and designers, use black ink or paint and vary the pressure of the brush. Write in a hurried fashion and allow the ink to run out as you're writing, creating variances in the shade of black. Try this technique with the appropriate media on lampshades, furniture, and picture frames, and in memory books.

I have bathed
in the poem
of the Ocean

Romantic
Calligraphy-Accented "Tiled" Mirror

A dding calligraphed quotations to a mirror's mat is a wonderful way to personalize home decorations. For this project, calligraphy is written on transparent vellum that is later decoupaged onto decorated mat "tiles"—a technique that results in layers of text and illustrations and makes it easy to begin a new lettered overlay if mistakes are made. Before beginning, test that the vellum and ink and the paste and varnish form a waterproof, bleedproof combination. Alternatively, use Joan's technique of transferring the finished calligraphy to the final paper overlay with a Gocco printer. Heavy printmaking or watercolor paper, cut into even tile squares to fit the mirror and frame, is decorated with botanical drawings. Joan drew the botanical illustrations herself, but you could use stamps or nature prints instead. The decorated mat tiles are pasted around the mirror, then the calligraphed overlay is pasted to the tiles with archival-quality stick flat paste. When dry, the mat is sealed with tinted varnish for added color.

Lettering Technique

Calligraphy created on transparent vellum paper can be pasted over decorated surfaces to add elegant written accents to projects.

For this project you will need:

- broad-edged pen nib for Italic calligraphy
- narrow-edged pen nib for Versal lettering
- calligraphy pen holder
- Italic hand lettering guide
- Versal lettering guide
- permanent, waterproof calligraphy ink in your desired colors
- transparent vellum or marking paper
- pencil
- botanical stamps or selected botanicals and stamping or printing inks
- heavy printmaking or watercolor paper
- archival quality stick flat paste
- mat knife, straight-edge, and cutting board
- mirror
- frame
- tinted varnish
- Gocco printer (optional)

the heritage of the past is the seed
that brings forth   NATIONAL
the harvest of the future.   ARCHIVES
BUILDING

1.

The   *that*   *the*

harvest of

harvest

harvest of

2.

future

3.

SEED VESSELS

4.

1. Refer to the Italic hand exemplar and ductus to begin. Lightly draw a baseline on vellum (or place the transparent vellum over a guideline template) and begin lettering your quotation with a broad-edged dip pen nib and waterproof calligraphy ink. Notice some special finishing touches: the Th ligature in "The" is created in one stroke (left). It is useful only where there is a capital T, where the crossbar is above the waistline, with a minuscule h, not with a minuscule t (right).

2. Three interesting things happen in the word combination "harvest of."

   The v tucks under the r (a). Because v has a diagonal stroke away from the r, if it were made in the usual manner (b), an undesirable white hole would disturb the rhythmic flow of the letters, drawing the eye to that spot. Therefore, the entrance serif on the v is eliminated and the first stroke is joined to the horizontal stroke of the r and actually curved slightly at the start to tuck it under.

   The s and t are joined by a decorative ligature done in one stroke. This could also be used with a ct combination.

   The bottom of the t drops below the baseline and ends in a wider than normal curve. This is strictly a decorative touch at the end of the word. The foot of the f in "of" is modified to end abruptly with a slight flick to the right (a). If it were to end in the normal curve to the left, it would create a conflict with the bottom of the t (c).

3. As "future" is the last word in the quotation, it ends with a flourish (a). This was done in one stroke, flattening the nib slightly to reduce the thickness of the stroke and turning it on its corner at the end.

4. The words "seed vessels" were lettered in Versals to complement the Italic lettering of the quotations. See the Versal lettering guide before beginning to letter with a narrow-edged pen nib and ink. The pairing of e's in "seed" is a perfect opportunity for a connecting stroke.

Romantic
Gilded Glass Coasters

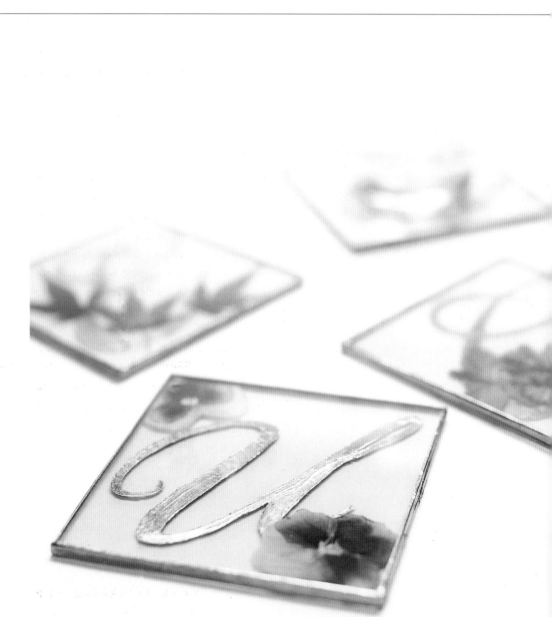

Add a personal twist to this popular coaster design by tracing and painting a beautiful script letter with glue and applying gold leaf or foil. These coasters are easily assembled by sticking two square pieces of glass together with copper metal tape. The gilded letter is on the top surface of the lower glass piece, and the pressed botanicals are set on top of the letter before the upper glass piece is sealed in place. Gilding also works well on paper and is a wonderful way to create personalized greeting cards and stationery.

For this project you will need:

8 square pieces of picture frame glass, corners sanded

copper metal tape, a self-adhesive tape used by stained glass artists

small pressed botanicals, such as flowers, leaves, and ferns

Bickham Script lettering guide

tracing paper

graphite transfer paper

pen

foil adhesive

brown craft acrylic paint (or any dark color)

small pointed brush

copper, gold, or silver foil or leaf

burnisher

stiff-bristled brush

soft cloth for burnishing tape onto glass edges

Lettering Technique

Beautiful script letters shine when gilded with gold, copper, or silver foil.

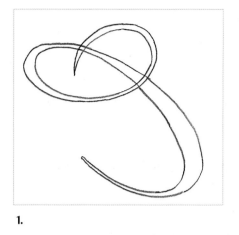

1.

1. Enlarge your desired Bickham Script letter to a suitable size to fit inside the glass squares. Trace the outlines of the letter onto tracing paper, then turn the paper over and retrace outlines to create a flopped reverse image of the letter. Transfer the reversed letter onto a square of glass with graphite transfer paper and a pen.

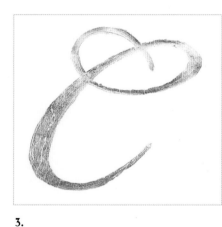

2.

2. Turn the glass over. You'll see a right-reading outline of the letter through the glass. Begin painting the letter with a small pointed brush and foil adhesive mixed with a drop of brown craft acrylic paint. Paint the outlines of the letter first, then flood the inside with the glue mixture. The glue will dry clear, so the added paint will help you see the letter while painting. Paint with smooth strokes to avoid brushmarks later in the transferred foil. Let the adhesive dry for approximately 20 minutes, then paint a second coat. Let dry another 20 minutes or until the glue is tacky.

3.

3. Apply the metal foil. If it is attached to a plastic backing, you'll need to burnish the metal sheet shiny-side up to the tacky glue surface. You can carefully lift the sheet during the burnishing process to see how the foil is transferring. For a smoother metal finish, use imitation gold leaf, a sheet of gold metal without a paper or plastic backing. Lay the leaf over the glue and press with your thumb over the letter outlines. Brush carefully with a stiff-bristled brush to remove excess leaf from the edges of the letters.

A B C D **Variation** Romantic script initials are not the only lettering style complemented by gilding. Use art deco letters for a strong graphic statement on personalized stationery or picture mats.

Romantic
Brush Script Monogrammed Napkins

These personalized napkins are a perfect introduction to brush calligraphy. Create these napkins as a perfect hostess gift or housewarming present, or use the lettering technique to decorate small pillows or to embellish other table linens, such as a tablecloth or a placemat set. Quick and smooth strokes are the key to creating polished lettering for the monograms. Make sure to purchase an extra napkin for practice while you're learning how to work with the fabric, brush, and paint. You can also create brush lettering with other paints and inks for use on paper, glass, and wood.

For this project you will need:

- purchased or handmade napkins
- Brush Script lettering guide
- small pointed (round) brush
- fabric paints in two coordinating colors
- iron to heat-set paint, if required

Lettering Technique

Creating script letters with a brush adds a personal touch to projects, and including an accent highlight or shadow is an opportunity to add more color to the project.

36

1.

1. Prewash the napkins to remove sizing. The following instructions are for specific letters—you'll find a ductus for all of the alphabet on page 20, but practice first with these step-by-step instructions to become comfortable with the lettering technique. The first stroke of S is made on the tip of the small pointed brush, pulling up from lower left to upper right in a quick motion. The second stroke curves around from the top in a reverse curve that follows through to the flourish. This stroke should also be made rapidly on the tip of the brush, applying some downward pressure in the swell of the curve. Highlights are made with a shade of the first color and should echo the stroke in shape and thickness. Keep some space between the highlight stroke and the letter stroke for a dimensional effect.

2.

2. To create a letter H, the first stroke is made holding the brush to the side of the stroke and, for clean terminals, giving the stroke a slight amount of pressure at the beginning and end. The second stroke is made more on the tip of the brush with a rapid movement, adding pressure for the second side of the H. For these strokes on the tip of the brush, hold the brush handle perpendicular to the paper. Highlight strokes are made with the lighter shade of paint and are thinner than the stroke they highlight, like a cast shadow. Highlight important structural parts of the letter, avoiding its decorative or fragile parts.

A B C D **Variation** The casual elegance of the blue napkins would coordinate well with delft dinnerware or other place settings. For special celebrations, create vibrant silk napkins with iridescent fabric paints. Make sure to heat set the fabric paint if necessary according to manufacturer's recommendations so that the monograms are permanent.

Romantic
"Stained-Glass" Travel Journal

This beautiful and elegant lettering is reminiscent of stained glass in its beautiful color fills and black outlines. Transferred gold leaf accents add to the classically romantic presentation. The letters are hand sketched and filled with many shades of three basic colors of watercolor pencils. Joan also adapted the lettering for a personal title page for the interior of the journal, which is shown here as a variation. A lovely addition to a travel memory book, this lettering style would also work well on greeting cards, a recipe book cover, a picture mat, or a calendar page.

For this project you will need:

- purchased memory book, or make your own with bookboard and marbleized paper
- tracing paper
- pencil
- transfer paper
- hot press (smooth) watercolor paper
- permanent archival-quality fine-point pigment liner pen in black
- watercolor pencils in multiple shades of blue, pink, and purple
- small flat brush
- imitation gold foil
- foil adhesive
- spray fixative (optional)
- PVA glue or other bookbinding glue

Lettering Technique

Loose, artistic sketches of letters look like stained glass when outlined with a fine marking pen and filled with watercolor pencils.

1.

2.

3.

4.

1. Sketch letters in pencil on tracing paper using loose, smooth strokes. Draw two types of capitals (such as Uncials, versals, or roman capitals) on top of each other, since the inner lines will look the most graceful if they are part of the letter rather than later additions. Study the roman letterforms in this book; notice the proportions of the letters and where the thick and thin lines occur. If necessary, enlarge and trace these letters to help you begin sketching.

2. When the letters are designed, draw a square around them smaller than the outside dimensions of the letters, and not overlapping the letter strokes. Embellish the letters with flourishes and diamond accents. Transfer lettering to the watercolor paper with transfer paper and a pencil. Redraw the outlines with a permanent fine black marking pen.

3. Fill in the sections of the letters and background with watercolor pencils, choosing multiple shades of each color for a rich look. Color lightly near the inside edges. Use a small flat brush with minimal water to spread and blend the watercolors.

4. Fill in diamonds with foil adhesive. When dry (clear), apply the foil according to manufacturer's directions. Spray the lettering with fixative (spray on a text scrap to check color shifts). Trim paper to a rectangle and attach to the travel journal with PVA glue or bookbinding glue.

 Variation These sketched letters are also beautiful without the boxed outline. In this form, they can easily be wrapped around a circle or on a curve and are perfect for many personalized paper crafts.

Sleek, clean, and stylish, modern lettering adds a contemporary and strong graphic presence to crafts. The term modern is commonly associated with sans-serif typefaces, though modern lettering also comprises hand-drawn letters, such as architect's printing, and even a style of roman type with serifs. The sans-serif typefaces have many subtle stylistic differences, and all have their own personality, particularly in the weight and width of strokes and in the geometric proportions of letters. Roman typefaces with serifs can become modern too, like Bodoni, with its exaggerated thick and thin strokes. The strongest feature of modern lettering is clean and smooth strokes. Lines are created with care by masking or stenciling, which also makes the letters suitable for etching and fabric transfer processes and other specialized treatments. Graphic shadow treatments are stylish embellishments to these clean letterforms. Most of these faces are created by outlining and filling the letters rather than by drawing them directly; this makes them perfect for projects that need strong initialing or labeling, such as kitchen canisters, frames, lampshades, and pillows. These letterforms work well with subtle, sophisticated color palates as well as with vibrant contrasting hues.

Architect's Hand

Drawn for this book by architect Gina M. Brown, the Architect's Hand is a modern and clean printing style created with a pencil. The rules are an integral part of the appearance—you'll need to use a straight-edge to create rules for the baseline, x-height, and capital height, as shown. Because the hand is capitals only, no descender guide rule is needed. Each stroke begins and ends with a strong backstroke to create a heavy terminal, and all vertical strokes are made by aligning the pencil with a straight-edge. Notice the personality of T and Y, as they sit slightly below the baseline. The heavier bold version is made by creating three parallel strokes that are clearly separated by white space. This style of lettering is perfect for embellishing house-warming gifts and new-home scrapbooks, conveying the impression of blueprints and architectural drawings.

© 2000 Gina M. Brown

Frutiger Black

Frutiger Black is a contemporary sans-serif typeface with simple and clean lines. It lends itself well to presentation as all lowercase letters, creating a bold, graphic element on crafts. Frutiger is particularly easy to trace and transfer; use the letters to create stencils for painting and etching glass, or for cutting out characters from paper to decoupage onto project surfaces.

ABCDEFGH
IJKLMNOPQ
RSUVWXYZ
abcdefghi
jklmnopqr
stuvwxyz
1234567890

© Adobe Systems Corporation

Futura®

Futura is classified as a geometric type, which means that the letterforms are based on geometric forms, such as the circle. Futura has very long ascenders and descenders, giving it a distinctive, elegant look that is perfect when combined with shadows (see page 58). Note the perfectly pointed tops to uppercase A and M.

ABCDEFGH
IJKLMNOPQ
RSUVWXYZ
abcdefghi
jklmnopqr
stuvwxyz
1234567890

© Adobe Systems Incorporated

Gill Sans® Light

Gill Sans, in its Light variation, is a versatile type with many distinctive applications. The lowercase a, with its penwriting influence, and the eyeglass-shaped lowercase g, make the typeface suitable for initialing purposes, as shown on page 52. It is an extremely wide face in its uppercase forms—pay attention, therefore, when using the capitals as initials; you might be surprised at how much space the letters can take!

ABCDEFGH
IJKLMNOPQ
RSUVWXYZ
abcdefghi
jklmnopqr
stuvwxyz
1234567890

© Adobe Systems Incorporated

ITC Anna® and Anna Pro®

Anna adds a splash of art-deco style to any project. This face offers alternative swash characters that form connecting strokes when combined judiciously—see page 56 for a presentation of the word *CAFE* with a connecting *A* and *F*. Art deco fonts combine simple geometric shapes into letterforms, echoing the age of flappers and jazz in the 1920s and 1930s and is particularly versatile when outlined and decoratively filled with color.

A A B C D E E

F F G H H I J K K

L M N O O P Q R R

S U V W W X Y Z

1 2 3 4 5 6 7 8 9 0

© 1991 and 1999 International Typeface Corporation

Bodoni

Bodoni represents the modern version of roman typefaces, which began near the end of the eighteenth century when advances in printing technology allowed type designers to contrast heavy stems with fine serifs and hairlines. Bodoni has quite a bit of personality—note the round finial ends on the lowercase letters—and makes a particularly elegant presentation with no embellishment added. See page 60 for a simple treatment of these letters.

A B C D E F G H
I J K L M N O P Q
R S U V W X Y Z

a b c d e f g h i
j k l m n o p q r
s t u v w x y z
1 2 3 4 5 6 7 8 9 0

© Adobe Systems Incorporated

Modern
Etched Glass Floating Frame

Create a personal collage of etched words on glass to frame a candid wedding picture for the perfect wedding, anniversary, or special-occasion gift. By composing each word separately and arranging them around your chosen photograph, you control the design and can plan a balanced arrangement. With a floating frame, lettering can be etched on both pieces of glass, creating dimension and sophistication. You can add typographic interest by experimenting with judicious combinations of text faces. *Note:* etching cream is caustic, so follow the manufacturer's safety directions carefully.

For this project you will need:

- double-paned floating glass frame
- lettering guides
- tracing paper
- transfer paper
- vinyl self-stick shelf lining paper
- etching cream
- straight-edge
- pencil
- fine-point black rolling ball pen
- craft knife
- low-tack masking tape
- foam brush
- glass cleaner

Planning a Layout

Spending time sketching thumbnails of possible layouts will help you create the perfect arrangement.

1.

2.

3.

1. Create thumbnails of possible lettering designs. Draw a small box in the same proportion as the image area of the frame. Mark the photograph's position and sketch your desired words in place. In the first sketch, the names were outlined in a lowercase sans-serif typeface for a modern appearance. An Italic ampersand connects the names, and a date was added. A quote from *Corinthians* was added in italic in the second sketch, and the names were rearranged. This sketch seemed awkward, so the more balanced third sketch was developed and accepted.

2. When you're fairly certain of your design, photocopy the chosen typefaces to the desired sizes. On a sheet of tracing paper, draw a baseline in pencil, then trace each word in pencil. Cut out each word to make collage pieces, and cut out a photo template. On another sheet of tracing paper, outline the inside dimensions of the frame for use as a template. Arrange the pieces on the frame template until you are satisfied with the final composition. Stick the pieces in place with low-tack masking tape, taking care that the tape does not block any of the letters.

3. Apply a piece of self-stick vinyl shelf liner to one side of the glass, smoothing out bubbles. Transfer the final lettering outlines from the tracing paper template to the vinyl with transfer paper and a pen. When all letters have been transferred, carefully cut out the inside of each letterform with a craft knife to expose areas of glass to be etched. Repeat for the front pane of glass if you've decided to place words there, too. Follow the etching cream manufacturer's directions to etch the exposed areas.

Variation Etch the surrounding glass instead of the letterforms; leave vinyl paper letterforms on the glass and remove vinyl paper surrounding them. When etching cream is removed, the words will be see-through in a field of frosted glass.

Modern
Architect's Blueprint Frame

What better way to present travel photos of architectural details than in a frame decorated with blueprint-style lettering? The technique shown here is created with a white colored pencil, but a blue pencil on cream paper would also be reminiscent of blueprints. The mat is bolted onto a thick plywood backing, continuing the modern architectural feel of the project. This lettering style would also be perfect in a scrapbook documenting your home's building process, on a picture mat framing a watercolor rendering of your home's entryway, or even on a greeting card to accompany a housewarming gift.

For this project you will need:

> matboard
>
> white colored pencil
>
> pencil sharper
>
> right triangle for
> vertical strokes and rules
>
> Architect's Hand lettering guide
>
> selected photographs
> of architectural details
>
> finishing washers
>
> flat-head Phillips wood screw
>
> thick plywood for backing
>
> electric drill
>
> small nail to create hole
> in mat for screw entry

Lettering Technique

While lettering, keep two white colored pencils handy—one well sharpened for the guide lines, and one dull for creating the heavier strokes of the letterforms.

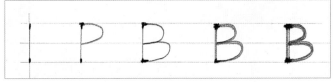

1.

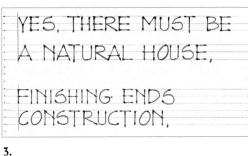

2.

3.

4.

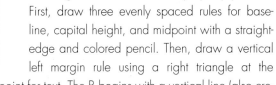

1. Creating the letterforms is a step-by-step process. First, draw three evenly spaced rules for baseline, capital height, and midpoint with a straightedge and colored pencil. Then, draw a vertical left margin rule using a right triangle at the starting point for text. The B begins with a vertical line (also created with a right triangle) placed right on the margin rule. Each letter should begin and end with a heavy backstroke, forming a distinctive terminal. The letters are complete with one set of strokes, but you can create a bold version by repeating each stroke three times in parallel, leaving a slight space between strokes.

2. The single strokes of letters work well in different sizes. Notice that the bars for capital A's appear at the midpoint between the baseline and midpoint rule. Also pay attention to other stylistic attributes, such as how the T and Y sit below the baseline to add character.

3. Vary the leading—the vertical space between baselines of words—to create visual balance between quotations. Make the space greater for an open and airy feel, or make the space tighter for a solid appearance. When spacing the quotations, look at the frame as a whole rather than in pieces. This is a good time to utilize a computer for planning purposes.

4. The quotation attributions are right-justified—they align on the right side. Begin each word with the last letter and print in order from right to left. The margin line, in this case, is on the right side.

 Variation The white pencil against a dark blue background creates a colorful setting for your photographs. Another option is a dark blue pencil on a cream background, which also mimics the appearance of architect's blueprints.

Modern
ABC Lamp Shades

This project is everything modern: bold colors, clean lettering, stylish lines. The strong shadow is broken away from the main letter, creating an empty moat of background color between shadow and letter. Painted lamp shades create subtle lighting effects in your home, shading and directing the light more completely than unpainted shades. The strong colors used here are perfect for a child's room, and you can add other accents in a similar style: paint an ABC border on the walls, paint letters on dresser drawers, or initials on a coat rack.

For this project you will need:

purchased lamp shades

Gill Sans Light lettering guide

tracing paper

white transfer paper

pen

acrylic paint in bright red, yellow-orange, dark violet, and white

foam brushes

small flat brush

small round brush

very small round brush or spotting brush

Lettering Technique

A border inserted between a letter and its shadow creates a stylish graphic element and another opportunity to add color to a design.

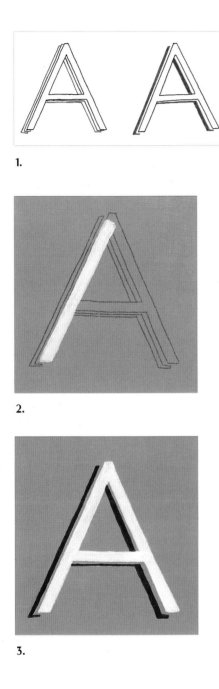

1.

2.

3.

1. Enlarge the Gill Sans Light letters to a size big enough to fill one face of a lamp shade. Check the size with the widest letter that you'll transfer; in this project the Gill Sans Light C is wider than the B and A. Outline the letter on tracing paper three times as shown, shifting the letter down and to the left each time (left). The outlines that create the final effect are the first letter and the final letter minus the area covered by the middle letter (right).

2. Transfer the final outlines to a lamp shade already base-coated with acrylic paint. White transfer paper is recommended because it's less messy than blue or graphite (though graphite paper is shown here for greater contrast). Center the letter carefully on the lamp shade face—each letter should sit on the same baseline for consistency, and the main (white) letter should be centered from side to side. Begin filling in the main letter with white acrylic paint and a small flat brush. *Tip:* Check the coverage of the base coat of paint by turning the lamp on with the shade in place. You'll immediately see areas that need more paint.

3. Continue painting the main letter with white paint, using a very small round or spotting brush to fill in detail in tight corners. You'll probably need to paint at least two or three coats of white for solid coverage over a darker color. Let dry. Paint the shadows with the base color used on another lamp shade panel and the small round brush. It's easy to correct mistakes with very small liner brush and the base color paint. When finished and completely dry, wipe with a damp soft cloth to remove transfer residue.

AB CD **Variation** The bright, playful colors shown here may not work with every decor! Try a subtle and sophisticated palette of moss green with gray-blue shadows in all lowercase letters for a more subdued accent piece.

Modern Sweetheart Sachets

These sachets are as sweet as the candy they're patterned after. This project utilizes a photocopy transfer process with wintergreen essential oil. Adding accent lines to the capital letters implies dimension, giving the words an incised appearance. Once you've drawn the letters in reverse, photocopy them on a common black and white copy machine. Then, use wintergreen essential oil and a burnishing tool to transfer the black carbon to fabric. This transfer technique also works well for curtains, pillows, even fabric purses, on any natural fabric—try using sheer chiffon for a layered effect.

For this project you will need:

- silk dupioni in yellow, pink, and green
- any lettering guide
- tracing paper
- fine black pigment marking pen
- access to a black and white photocopier
- wintergreen essential oil
- cotton balls
- burnishing tool (or back of spoon)
- scissors
- cream satin cording
- thread
- sewing machine
- sachet filling such as lavender, rose petals, or potpourri

Lettering Technique

Wintergreen essential oil transfers the black toner from photocopies of reversed lettering onto fabric. Accent lines added to letters implies dimension.

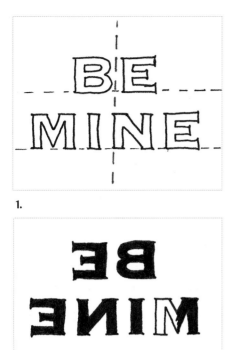

1.

1. Draw a heart on tracing paper to use as a sewing pattern. Enlarge your desired lettering guide to the correct size to fit well inside your drawn heart. Draw a baseline on another piece of tracing paper, and outline phrases such as "be mine," "I'm yours," "true love," or "kiss me." Stack the words on two lines centered one above the other, as shown. To center, draw the words separately, then paste one above the other following a lightly sketched center rule (the red line in the illustration).

2.

2. Turn the tracing paper over and retrace the letters so that they're reversed. Fill in the letters completely with a black permanent marking pen, being careful to choose a pen that doesn't bleed or feather on the tracing paper. Fill in the letters as evenly and completely as possible. If you make a mistake, correct it directly on the tracing paper with correction fluid or white opaque gouache made for correcting graphic design layouts. If you have access to a black and white photocopier that has a reverse option, you can skip this step and fill in the original right-reading letters sketched in step 1.

3.

3. Draw shadow outline accents to each letter. The arrow shows the direction of the light, so the shadows appear on the right and bottom sides of letters. If you can't imagine where the lines should be placed, you might find it easier to place them on the right-reading side first, then retrace them on the back. Photocopy the final lettering on a black and white copier. Place the lettering toner-side down on fabric. Soak the back of the lettering with a cotton ball dipped in wintergreen essential oil. Burnish the back of the damp photocopy with a burnishing tool or the back of a spoon until the design is transferred. Lift an edge of the photocopy periodically to check the transfer process, being careful to replace the paper exactly. When transferred to your satisfaction, let dry. Transfers may not hold the same detail on synthetic fabrics; test on a swatch first. When complete, cut and sew the sachets, filling them with potpourri.

A B C D **Variation** This image transfer process holds detail surprisingly well. Experiment with inside lines, filling in the letters with a pattern or adding embellishments and flourishes. This technique can be used to accent any fabric project, including quilting squares and fabric-covered lamp shades.

Modern
Cloisonné-Style Coffeepot

A rt-deco-inspired lettering is the perfect foil for this technique to create imitation cloisonné. The clean period design is accented by outlining the letters with thick, metallic oven-firing porcelain paint that is applied from a nozzled tube. A wash of transparent color to fill adds to the effect. Creating smooth lines with the paint tube may take a bit of practice, but when you've become comfortable with the process, you can apply this technique to ceramic tiles, decorative plates, or any porcelain, ceramic, or glass surface that can withstand oven firing.

For this project you will need:

purchased porcelain
or ceramic coffeepot

ITC Anna Pro lettering guide

tracing paper

graphite transfer paper

pen

copper water-based
oven-firing cloisonné outline
paint in a nozzled tube
(Pebeo Porcelaine 150 paints
work well, but any ceramic
paint that imitates stained-glass
leading will work)

light green semi-opaque
water-based oven-firing paint
for ceramics

small pointed natural-hair brush

alcohol to clean coffeepot

Lettering Technique

Art-deco lettering outlined with
a thick metallic oven-firing paint,
then filled with a transparent
wash, imitates enamel.

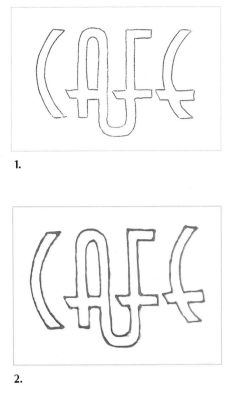

1.

2.

1. Enlarge the ITC Anna Pro lettering guide to your chosen size. Outline the letters CAFE on tracing paper, using the special swash capitals. Notice how the A and the F connect, adding a stylish design element. Transfer the letters to your coffeepot (already degreased with alcohol) with graphite transfer paper and a pen. Placement of the lettering is important—letters should be well centered between the spout and handle and the lid and bottom. If placement is not correct, wash it off and transfer the letters again. *Tip:* If you have to retransfer your lettering, use a different color pen on the tracing paper so you can easily tell what outlines you've already traced.

2. Outline each letter with the cloisonnè outlining paint, using even pressure and smooth motions while squeezing the tube. Practice creating a smooth, clean line on scrap paper first. Outline each part of the letter as a segment, stopping at the corners. Turn the coffeepot while outlining so your hand is always in a comfortable position, but be careful where you rest your palm—you don't want to smudge the paint or transfer lines. If you make a mistake, you can remove the paint with water or alcohol and a cotton swab. Don't worry too much about uneven coverage, as the outlines will melt slightly and even out a bit in the oven. Let dry.

3. Fill the insides of each letter with a wash of light green ceramic paint and a small brush. Use a natural-hair brush for smooth paint coverage without hard brushstrokes. The color does not need to be a solid fill, as the paints are semitransparent. If you try to fix a mistake at this stage, be careful not to ruin the copper outline work you've already completed. When finished, let dry 24 hours and follow manufacturer's recommendations for heat setting in the oven.

3.

A B C D **Variation** Instead of using the clean art-deco letters chosen for this project, try a more ornate Victorian-inspired design. Add your own embellishments to the feet and crossbar with the cloisonnè paint to give the letter personality. Try this painting technique on canisters, sugar and cream containers, or any glass or ceramic surface that can be oven fired.

Modern
Shadowed Letter Canisters

A set of ceramic canisters is made modern with the addition of deep painted shadows that merely hint at the letterform creating them. A simple and bold color scheme and wide letter spacing add to the strong graphic effect. Sharp edges and smooth paint coverage are the keys to this decorative technique, so a mask is made from self-adhesive vinyl paper before applying the paint. Try this lettering style on glass or ceramic vases, kitchen cabinet doors, or any project that would be enhanced by a modern-styled label.

For this project you will need:

ceramic canister set

Futura lettering guide

solvent-based air-drying paint for ceramics (Pebeo Ceramique works well)

vinyl self-stick shelf lining paper or airbrush masking film

disposable medium-pointed brush, or medium-pointed brush and turpentine brush cleaner

tracing paper

transfer paper

pen

craft knife

Lettering Technique

Invisible letterforms are defined by their shadows in this technique for creating deep, modern dimension.

1. Enlarge the lettering guide to your chosen size. Draw a baseline on tracing paper. Trace the letters onto tracing paper and fill them in. Use a wide letter spacing, both to create a modern look and to allow space for a large shadow. These letters are the white space of the final letterforms—they provide a boundary only and won't be painted.

1.

2. Place the tracing paper over the lettering guide again, but so that the next set you trace is evenly shifted down and to the right. Trace the letters and fill them in; this step is represented in black in this example. Draw connecting lines (dashed blue lines) between the original letters and the second set of letters at corresponding outside points. Not all points will need to be connected—with experience, you'll develop a feel for which ones are necessary.

2.

3. Fill in the areas defined by the second set of letters and the interior of the connecting lines up to the border of the original letters. This will result in a deep shadow that, when the original set of letters is deleted, becomes the shadowed design. Transfer these shadow forms with transfer paper onto vinyl self-stick shelf lining paper that has already been smoothly applied to the ceramic canister. Cut out the shadow areas from the vinyl with a craft knife, using clean, sharp lines. Apply the paint according to manufacturer's directions; when paint has partially set, remove the vinyl paper quickly and smoothly. Small mistakes can be corrected with solvent and a cotton swab when wet, or by carefully scraping them off with a razor blade when dry.

3.

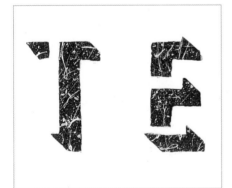

**AB
CD** **Variation** Because the unpainted area of the canister is masked, many decorative painting techniques can be utilized on the letters. Try spotting a contrasting shade of paint over the first shade by loading a stiff paintbrush or old toothbrush with paint and flicking the bristles with a gloved finger. Or, try sponging a complementary color over the base coat.

Initialed Shaker Boxes

I t may be a gift to be simple, but it isn't always easy—a single lower-case letter against a solid background leaves no place to hide mistakes! These classic Shaker boxes are painted with milk paint, a dead-flat finishing paint made from one of the oldest paint recipes known. Bodoni, the typeface used here, is one of the first modern typefaces developed—the accentuated difference between the line weights and serifs of each letter makes them stylistically beautiful without adornment. Choose c for cosmetics, s for safety pins, or pick a letter simply because it's beautiful.

For this project you will need:

- unfinished wooden Shaker boxes
- Bodoni lettering guide
- milk paint in two colors
- transfer paper
- pen
- foam brushes
- disposable container for mixing paint
- medium-sized sable flat brush
- small round sable brush
- fine sandpaper
- sealer

Lettering Technique

Stylistically beautiful single lowercase letters create a strong graphic presence.

60

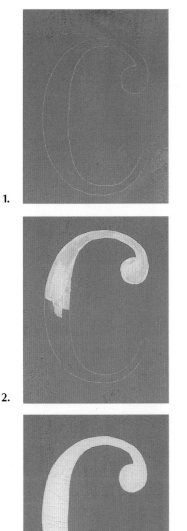

1. Following manufacturer's directions for mixing and applying milk paint, paint the boxes with a base coat of paint and a foam brush. In the example, one coat of the darker shade of paint was enough, but the lighter paint needed two coats for even coverage. Let dry completely. Enlarge your chosen Bodoni lowercase letter to the correct size to fit on the box's lid. Transfer the letter to the lid with either white or graphite transfer paper, depending on the darkness of your chosen background. Try to keep the transfer lines just within the letter's border so the lines will not show on the finished box.

2. Mix the milk paint for the letterform. Using a sable flat brush, begin filling in the letterform. Avoid loading the brush with too much paint. Turn the box and the brush edge to create a sharp border for the letter. Fill in corner details with a small round brush. Continue applying a light coat of paint until the letter is filled. The paint will dry unevenly at first, so don't worry if coverage is not perfect on the first coat. Be careful not to rest your hand on the working surface while painting.

3. When the first coat is complete, let dry completely. Lightly sand any bubbles in the paint. Add a second light coat of paint to the letter, let dry, and, if necessary, add a third. Be careful to keep coats light and to let them dry well between applications, or cracks may appear (though cracks can look good, too!). When the lettering is complete and dry, sand the box with fine sandpaper to add distressed edges and to even any dried paint bubbles. Finish with a sealer such as Danish oil.

ABCD Variation Using two tints of wood stain also works well on Shaker boxes. Because stain is so fluid, create a boundary between the letter and the background by etching a border line on the wooden lid around the letter with a craft knife for sharp definition between stained areas. Alternatively, try painting masking fluid (an easily removed liquid mask) around the letterform for a softer border between stain tints.

Decorative Lettering

nything goes with decorative lettering! This chapter encompasses not only embellished watercolor-filled alphabets but letters formed with unusual tools, surprising and playful fills, embossed details, letters created with plaster, and cut-out letterforms decoupaged onto wooden bowls. Decorative lettering can mean using traditional letters in a special way, or it could mean creating an alphabet all your own. Color, color, color fills these styles, and whimsy and fun are the order of the day. No other style of lettering allows as much freedom to personalize your crafts with poems, phrases, labels, or even special Chinese calligraphy. The suggestions on the following pages are not only perfect for vases, journals, lamp shades, and bowls but also are great for any decorative purpose. Try the techniques on frames, clocks, canisters, birdhouses—even the walls of your home.

Crystal Onyx

Lettering artist Margaret Lammerts created this fun and creative alphabet especially for this book and incorporated it into her garden journal, featured on page 70. Copy and trace it exactly as shown, filling the insides of the letters with watercolors or other media, or use the alphabet to inspire your own designs. The square template (left) can be cut from plastic film to use as a guide to creating the background boxes for filling.

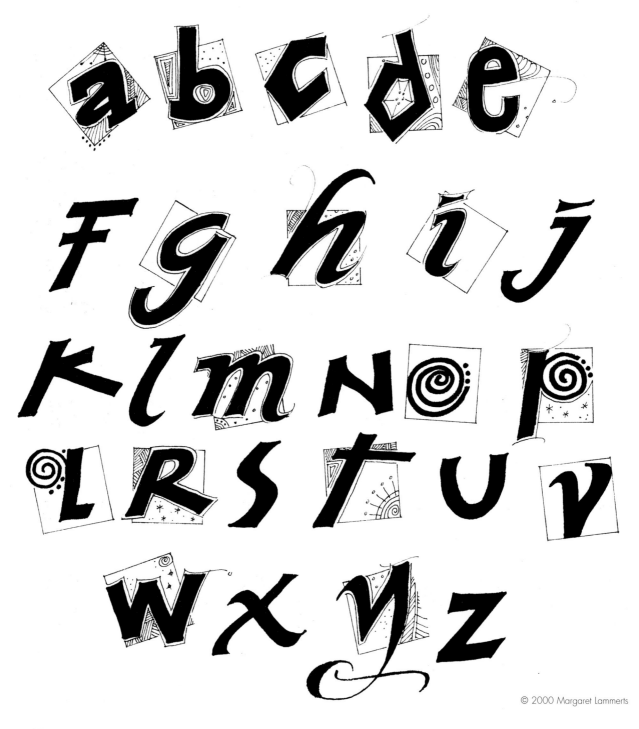

© 2000 Margaret Lammerts

Party™

Party combines wild abandon with classic script calligraphy. You can trace and fill these computer-generated letters or use a pointed pen or brush to create them from scratch. The eclectic letters are perfect for vases, memory books, party invitations and place cards, or any other project with a lighthearted theme.

A B C D E F G H
I J K L M N O P Q
R S U V W X Y Z

a b c d e f g h i j k l m
n o p q r s t u v w x y z

1 2 3 4 5 6 7 8 9 0

© 1993 International Typeface Corporation

Algerian Condensed

Influenced by nineteenth-century Victorian woodcuts, Algerian Condensed is a computer-generated type-face that adds a distinctive look to any project. Paint the shadow lines with a contrasting shade for colorful craft labels. The numbers are particularly stylish and would make a good accent for lamp shades and clocks.

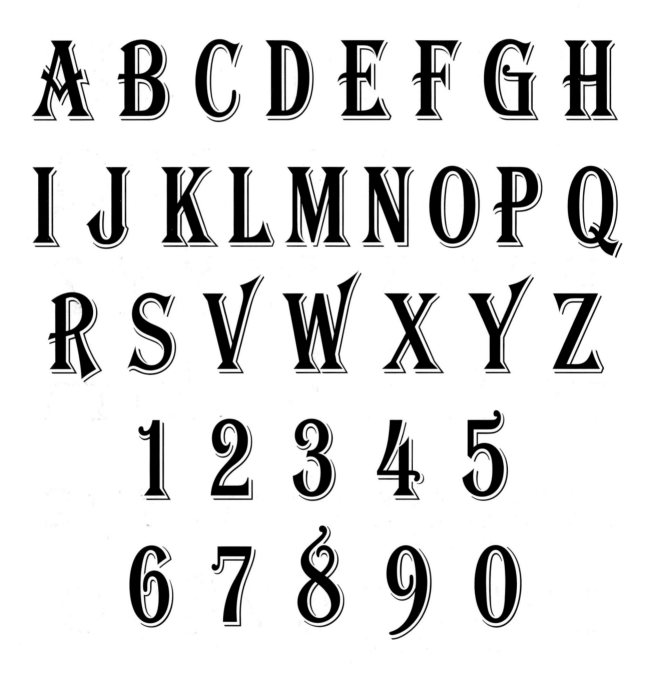

© 1988 International Typeface Corporation

ITC Obelisk™ Light

A casual but elegant computer-generated typeface, Obelisk is patterned after chiseled lettering rather than handwriting. Its informal style would add a trendy feel to lettering projects such as canisters, vases, and memory books. Jumble the letters a bit to create a 1950s appearance.

ABCDEFGH
IJKLMNOPQ
RSUVWXYZ
abcdfghijklm
nopqrstvwxyz
1234567890

© 1996 International Typeface Corporation

ITC Rennie Mackintosh™ Light

Another typeface influenced by architect printing, ITC Rennie Mackintosh is based on the lettering of Scottish designer Charles Rennie Mackintosh. Two forms are shown—a less ornamented version on left and a narrower and more stylish version on the right where available. This lettering style would complement projects designed in the popular arts-and-crafts style.

A A B B C D E F
G G H H I J K L L
M M N O O O P Q Q
R R S S U V
W W X Y Z
1 2 3 4 5 6 7 8 9 0

© 1996 International Typeface Corporation

ITC Vintage™

Simple and elegant, this computer-generated typeface is reminiscent of magazine type from the early twentieth century. Easy to trace and embellish, the thicks and thins are almost calligraphic in style. Use this face to label ceramic pieces such as cream and sugar bowls, to decorate memory books, or to cut from vinyl to create a mask for glass etching on vases and frames.

ABCDEFGH
IJKLMNOPQ
RSUVWXYZ

ABCDFGHIJ
KLMNOPQR
STUVWXYZ
1234567890

© 1996 International Typeface Corporation

Decorative GARDEN JOURNAL

R ecord your garden's yearly progress in this playfully lettered garden journal. Your imagination can run wild when filling these letters with watercolors—experiment with colors and applications, and always remember that there are no mistakes! This eccentric and creative lettering technique allows much flexibility in filling and ornamenting, not to mention in adding special letters all your own. For example, Margaret replaced the o in Journal with a flower—an appropriate botanical addition!

For this project you will need:

purchased scrapbook, or make your own with bookboard and pastepaper, as shown

Crystal Onyx lettering guide

extra-fine waterproof archival-quality black marker

hot-pressed (smooth) watercolor paper

watercolors (either tube or cake is fine)

small pointed watercolor brushes

palette

Lettering Technique

Whimsical outlined letters are filled with a creative combination of watercolors, and selected letters are replaced with appropriate icons.

1.

2.

3.

1. Sketch the basic letterforms with a pencil on watercolor paper. Use Margaret's specially designed alphabet on page 64 as inspiration only, or trace and transfer the actual letters for your project. When the letters are drawn to your satisfaction, outline them with an extra-fine waterproof black marker. Add double outlines to the letters to form a white inline, if desired. Look for a letter to substitute with an icon, such as the flower, shown here, that replaces the o.

2. Draw boxes of an even size behind the letters. In a small palette, mix watercolors of your choosing, or use cake watercolors and clean water. Flood each letter with a selected color using a small pointed watercolor brush. Paint just one letter at a time while discovering all the blending possibilities that you can create with watercolors. Try flooding a letter with clean water only first, then lightly placing one drop each of two colors on the wet letter—the paint will spread throughout the water, forming a subtle blended fill. Fill the letters with two shades of the same color for depth, or overpaint a color with an accent of another color.

3. Finally, when the letters are completely dry, add accents and flourishes with your extra-fine waterproof black marker to embellish the interior of the background squares. Draw stars, geometric patterns, dots, stripes, curves—whatever strikes your fancy!

A B C D **Variation** Choose a more limited palette to coordinate the lettering to your decor. Here, French country colors of green, blue, and yellow were chosen for a recipe book to complement the kitchen. You could also fill these letters with watercolor markers, pencils, pastels, or even crayons.

Decorative
DOTTED GRADIENT DESSERT PLATES

These eclectic letters combine a whimsical and playful dotted fill with a traditional and classical letterform. Similar to pointillism, a French postimpressionist painting technique, each letter is composed of dots of color that blend into a harmonious presentation. Personalize your dishes with a short word like cake, or use your initials as the letter choices. This project is also an introduction to reverse painting, as the dots of oven-firing gloss enamel fill in reversed letterforms from the underside, leaving the eating area smooth and clean.

For this project you will need:

4 clear glass dessert plates

oven-firing gloss acrylic enamel in three shades of green (paint should be used only on surfaces that will not come into contact with food)

letters C, A, K, E in selected typeface

graphite tracing paper

pen

transfer paper

china marker

paintbrush with round handle end

palette

Lettering Technique

Create shading by filling letterforms with shades of stippled dots that blend into each other.

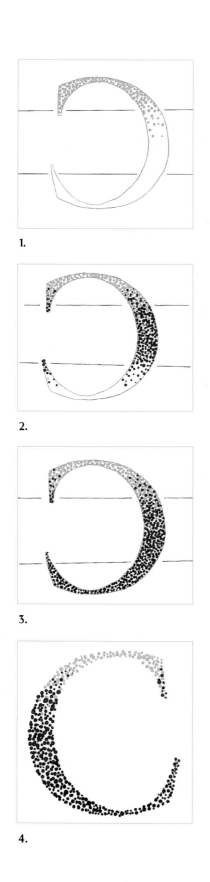

1.

2.

3.

4.

1. Enlarge the letters to fit on the dessert plates. Transfer them onto the front of one dessert plate, slightly off center and off an edge. Mark two horizontal guidelines on the front with a china marker to indicate the placement of the color breaks. Pour a small amount of the lightest enamel paint onto a palette. Turn one plate over so that the letter outline is backwards and begin to paint the top section of the letter. Dip the small rounded end of a paintbrush handle into the paint and fill in the outlined area by creating dots with a pouncing motion, reloading as needed. Fill in the edges of the letter first, then the center. Space the dots close to each other at the top of the letter but begin to space them wider around the marked midpoint guide to allow space for the next shade of green. Repeat this step for each plate, then let dry completely before continuing.

2. Pour a small amount of the medium shade of green enamel paint onto the palette and begin filling in the middle section of the letterform. Overlap the lighter area slightly before using the solid medium shade only. Space the dots wider as the bottom guide is reached. Repeat this step for each plate, then let dry completely before continuing.

3. Pour a small amount of the dark shade of green enamel paint onto the palette and fill in the bottom section of the letter with dots. Overlap the medium green area slightly before using the solid dark shade only. Repeat this step for each plate, then let dry completely.

4. When painting is complete, clean off graphite tracing lines and guidelines, then cure and oven fire the plates according to paint manufacturer's directions. When the plate is viewed from the surface, the right-reading letter will show through.

A B C D **Variation** Instead of creating a blend of shades, fill in the letterform with random dots of three colors to match the palette of your dining room's decor. The confetti-like fill resembles a pebbled mosaic and would be lovely on a glass vase or on monogrammed napkins.

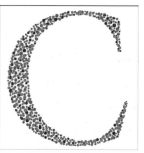

Decorative
ABC-XYZ Embossed Portfolio

T he dynamic and spontaneous letterforms created with a ruling pen are enhanced by embossing their outlines on this homemade portfolio. A ruling pen is traditionally used for drafting technical drawings, but the unpredictable and expressive letters it allows make it a favorite with calligraphers as well. Cindy used nature prints of two Canadian grasses, rough fescue and cord grass, to create the strong, graphic patterns on the edge of the portfolio. The back of her portfolio holds a surprise: the letters ABC XYZ embellished exactly as on the front, but in reverse!

For this project you will need:

purchased portfolio,
or materials to make your own

ruling pen

black calligraphy ink

drawing paper

transfer paper

pen

acrylic paint in pearl gold

pointed brush

embossing pen

gold embossing paper

heat gun

Lettering Technique

A dynamic presentation of lettering becomes even stronger with the addition of embossed gold outlines.

1.

1. Load a ruling pen with ink and sketch the letters *ABC XYZ* on drawing paper. Create many sketches, using spontaneous and strong strokes, stylish accents, and doubled lines for a bold effect. It may take a few tries to become familiar with all the possibilities that a ruling pen can offer, but it's well worth the effort. When you're happy with a sketch, draw diamond accents where desired.

2. Enlarge your lettering on a photocopier to fill the portfolio face. Transfer the outlines of the lettering to the portfolio with transfer paper and a pen.

3. Fill in the letters with pearl gold acrylic paint and a pointed brush. Try to keep the rough edges and variable line weights that the ruling pen created. Use smooth, clean strokes to avoid showing brush marks.

2.

4. Outline the letters with an embossing pen. (This is a pen that deposits a clear slow-drying liquid that bonds embossing powder to the drawn lines.) Sprinkle embossing powder on the pen lines and tap off the excess powder (reserve the extra powder for later use). Heat the letters with a heat gun according to manufacturer's directions until the powder melts.

3.

4.

AB CD **Variation** While the gold-on-gold paint and embossing powder combination used here is sophisticated, you can change the mood of the lettering by using different combinations, such as this masculine combination of copper embossing over dark blue ink.

Raised Chinese Calligraphy Lamp Shade

Decorative

G ive Chinese calligraphy a new dimension with this technique for creating plaster relief characters from joint compound accented with a homemade glaze. The dark glaze ages the calligraphy, emphasizing the texture of the plaster letters. These ancient characters, cho and raku, mean "long, lengthy" and "comfort, relief, pleasant, joyful," and, when combined mean "long happiness"—a perfect sentiment for your home. Use this technique to decorate picture frames, lamp shades, jewelry boxes, or even to add a frieze to your living-room walls.

For this project you will need:

- lamp and lamp shade
- Chinese characters
- small container of joint compound or drywall mud
- off-white craft acrylic paint
- burnt sienna craft acrylic paint
- acrylic gloss medium
- acetate for stencil
- transfer paper (white if acetate is colored, blue it acetate is clear)
- craft knife
- fine pen
- quick-release tape
- spray temporary adhesive
- putty knife
- straight-edge razor blade
- foam brush
- soft rag

Glazed Lettering

When cutting the outline of each character, don't cut too perfectly. Try to keep the rough brushlines intact.

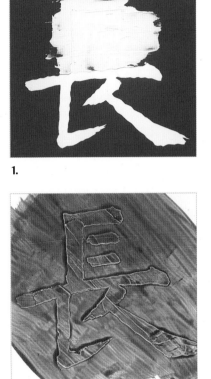

1.

2.

3.

template

1. Photocopy the Chinese characters to the desired size, then create a stencil by transferring the outlines to acetate using transfer paper and a pen. Cut out the outlines of each character with a craft or stencil knife. Spray the back of the stencil with temporary adhesive and place it on the lamp shade, securing it with quick-release tape. Using smooth strokes and a putty knife, apply a thin layer of joint compound to the exposed areas of the stencil. Stroke marks and other variations in the plaster's finish will add dimension and enhance the calligraphy. When all areas are covered, remove the stencil. Clean any mistakes with a straight-edged razor blade and let dry thoroughly.

   Using a foam brush, paint the shade with two coats of craft acrylic paint, letting the paint dry between coats. Let dry completely.

2. Make a glaze by mixing approximately two parts acrylic gloss medium with one part burnt sienna craft acrylic. Test the color intensity on a piece of scrap cardboard painted with your base color, and add more paint to tint if needed. Apply the glaze with a foam brush to the lamp shade, allowing it to collect at the edges of the plaster.

3. Working quickly, wipe the glaze with a soft, clean rag or paper towel, using a circular motion to create a texture. Leave as much color as possible at the edges of the raised lettering to enhance its dimension. Because the glaze can set quickly, complete steps 3 and 4 in two stages for the front and back of the lamp shade. Keep the borders of each section slightly irregular so that overlapping edges of wet and drying glazes don't create a visible line.

ABCD **Variation** Experiment with combinations of base and glaze colors to suit the mood of the piece or your home's decor. Here a base color of red oxide acrylic was combined with a burnt umber glaze and a base of interference (metallic) green acrylic combined with a black glaze. Alternatively, instead of aging the lettering with a dark glaze, try a burnt umber acrylic base with highlights added by rubbing on a gold metallic wax.

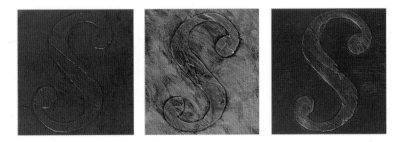

"Eat Your Peas" Decoupage Bowls

Hand-drawn letters, cut out of vibrant decorative paper and decoupaged onto wooden bowls, offer a commanding yet playful voice in your kitchen. These humorous decorative bowls are perfect to hang in a row over a kitchen window, by the dinner table, or even in a child's room. The bright painted background was created with animators' vinyl paint, a bright, highly pigmented paint used to color cartoon cels. Decoupaged letters work well with many crafts—try jewelry boxes, serving trays, frames, even furniture. Another appropriate phrase? How about "Call your mother!"

For this project you will need:

3 small wooden bowls

animators' vinyl paint (or acrylic paint) in your desired colors

round and flat paintbrushes

tracing paper

pencil

transfer paper

artists' colored paper in two shades (origami paper or graphic artists' color swatch paper works well)

craft knife

white craft glue

decoupage medium

foam brush

fine sandpaper

Lettering Technique

Playful hand-drawn letters become bright and dimensional when cut from colored paper and decoupaged on a wooden surface.

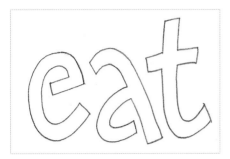

1.

1. Sketch your desired letters on tracing paper. Janet used simple lower-case forms so they would have nice, clean lines. Notice how the strokes of the e and the a don't close the letterform—this looks contemporary and playful, and adds a dynamic variation when pasted on top of the more solid backing letter. Don't worry about lining the letters evenly on a baseline; they'll look more interesting if they're jumbled a bit, and you'll be cutting them out separately, anyway.

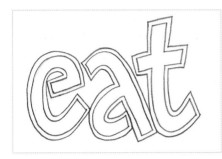

2.

2. When you have the letters drawn to your satisfaction, sketch an outline around the whole letter. Try to keep a regular space between the inside and outside letterforms, and fill in the closing strokes of the letters, if desired. With transfer paper and a pen, transfer the inside lines to the light shade of artists' colored paper, and transfer the outside lines to a darker shade of artists' colored paper. Cut out the letters from the colored paper with a craft knife. There's no need to cut perfectly straight lines—variations in stroke thickness add to the handmade look of the final piece.

3.

3. Glue the letters onto prepainted wooden bowls with white craft glue. Paste the larger, darker letters first, then paste the smaller, lighter letters on top. Place the letters in a dynamic arrangement, with some letters leaning left and others leaning right for variation. Let dry completely. Apply four to five coats of decoupage medium to each bowl according to manufacturer's directions, letting dry and lightly sanding between coats with fine sandpaper for a smooth finish.

A B C D **Variation** The strong solid colors used in the project are a perfect complement to the decorative painting in the bowls, but for a project using letters only, try decorating the inside letters with permanent markers or paint before decoupaging them to the craft surface. Test your chosen colors with decoupage medium before using it on the final project to be sure they are color fast.

Decorative
PAINTED GLASS VASE

This wild yet sophisticated vase is created with water-based glazes that are heat-set in your oven. Lisa drew many sketches on tracing paper before deciding on the final lettering design. When she was satisfied, she used her tracing paper as a template by inserting it into the vase and securing it to the side with masking tape so that the lettering showed through the glass. She used a medium round brush to create the lettering, which allowed her to develop dramatically contrasting thick and thin strokes. This dynamic lettering technique can be adapted to any medium and surface, so try it on kitchen canisters, pillows, and greeting cards with the appropriate ink or paint.

For this project you will need:

clear glass vase

transparent and semi-opaque water-based oven-firing paints for glass surfaces in your desired colors (Pebeo Porcelaine 150 works well, but any oven-firing enamel would work)

medium round brush

tracing paper

pencil

masking tape

paper towel

hair dryer

Lettering Technique

Using a medium round brush, you can create lettering with pronounced thick and thin lines. Sketch your designs on tracing paper to finalize a look before painting.

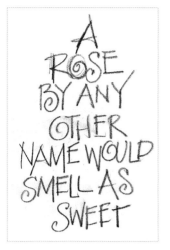

1.

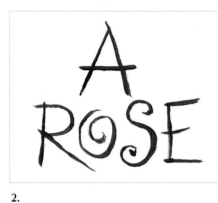

2.

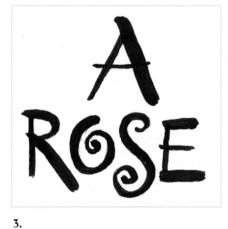

3.

1. Sketch your phrase on tracing paper with a pencil. Look at different ways that the letters can be combined—for example, the double L combination in "smell" can be nested, and the D in "would" looks great sitting inside the L. Creating a swirl for the letter O complements the rose swirls decorating the outside of the vase. By not restricting the letters to a single baseline, you can create dynamic combinations, as was done here for the words "rose" and "name."

2. Test the paints on glass to check colors, opacity, lettering, and layering before painting your final project—you can easily clean the paints off with soap and water if they haven't been heat set. Apply a diluted base coat to the glass with crumpled paper towel, if desired, and let dry. Insert your tracing paper template into the vase where desired and tape in place. Use the tip of a medium round brush and follow the template to paint the outlines of the letters. Because you're working on a rounded surface, you may find it advantageous to speed the drying of the paint with a hair dryer to prevent drips and smudges.

3. Emphasize selected strokes of the letters by painting them in heavier lines using the same round brush, but with more pressure. Let dry. Embellish the vase as desired with swirls and stripes, let dry, and oven fire according to manufacturer's recommendations.

AB CD **Variation** The one-color presentation of the lettering is perfect for this highly decorated presentation. For projects where lettering is the only decoration, try filling in random heavy strokes with polka dots in a contrasting color. This would be an eye-catching accent for lamp shades and painted wall borders.

Decorative
Playful Herb Pots

O n their own, old-style roman letters are classical and traditional, but mix them up, add a shadow, and they become playful and fun! A collage of upper- and lowercase letters gains depth with shadows that imply a variety of letter levels. The letters are painted with craft acrylics specially formulated for use on terra cotta. The effect is a subtle wash of color rather than a bold statement, but you can always try brighter colors for flowerpots. This dynamic presentation of words is also wonderful for canisters, vases, memory book covers, or anywhere a lively accent is appropriate.

For this project you will need:

terra cotta pots

Caslon or Bodoni lettering guide

tracing paper

graphite transfer paper

pen

craft acrylic paints for terra cotta in cream, rust, and teal

small chisel-edged brush

small liner brush

fine sandpaper

soft rag

Lettering Technique

A playful combination of upper- and lowercase letters with varying shadows adds whimsy to simple words.

1. Enlarge your chosen roman lettering guide to the desired size. The upper- and lowercase letters are used at the same relative size in these examples. Trace the letters onto tracing paper, but don't keep the letters on the same baseline. Mix them in a collage pattern and choose one letter to be lowercase—pick a letter that has a lot of character, such as the g shown here. Overlap the letters slightly in a pleasing pattern. You may want to try a number of combinations before you settle on one style.

1.

2. Add a shadow to each letter in the direction of the arrow. The shadow form is simply the same shape as the letterform, with a diagonal connection between corresponding outside edges of the original letterform and its shadow, as shown. Have the shadows overlap the next letter to create a multilevel dimension that adds to the playful attitude. Transfer the final outlines to the pots (which you've already given a color wash of cream, rust, and teal paint with a soft rag) with graphite transfer paper.

2.

3. Fill in the original letterforms with cream paint using a small chisel-edged brush. Turn the brush as needed to utilize its edge to create a sharp definition to the letters. You'll probably need to apply two coats of paint for full coverage. When dry, fill in the shadow area with rust paint and a small liner brush. Use smooth, clean strokes; apply a second coat for additional coverage if necessary. When dry, sand lightly across the letters with fine sandpaper for a distressed effect.

3.

A B C D **Variation** Add horizontal strokes in white paint with a small liner brush to increase the playful aspect of the letters. Also add a highlight stroke along the edge of the light side (directly opposite the shadow side), to further define the letterforms.

Vintage Lettering

A

B

C

Vintage lettering recalls a time gone by, of ancestors, history, and memories. Vintage alphabets include the truly old Versals, a hand-lettered, all-capital alphabet created by outlining and filling letters with a narrow-edged calligraphy pen or pointed brush, and chunky Uncials with a Celtic feel, as well as typefaces influenced by Roman carvings and early forms of movable type, such as Caslon. Lettering can be made vintage by adding period embellishments or by treating the letterforms with chemicals to rust them. Alternatively, you can glue together cutout letters to create a charcoal rubbing. Pillows, placemats, curtains, clocks, and other home decorating accents can be created using old-style lettering. You'll find more vintage-influenced alphabets in the Decorative Lettering chapter.

Traditional Versals

Versals are a historic form of capital letters (majuscules). Unlike other calligraphic hands, such as Italic and Foundation, which are created by connecting strokes that make the letters in segments, Versals are created by outlining and filling, layering strokes with a narrow-edged calligraphy pen or brush. They are so named because they were originally used to begin verses. The Traditional Versal is ornate and elegant, and the Modern Versal is formal and classic. You can use these letters as outlines only, outlined and filled with another color, or in a solid color. They are also appropriate for gilding. Try them on scarves, lampshades, curtains (see page 96), and decorative wall borders.

©2000 Lisa Engelbrecht

Modern Versals

30°
pen angle

Modern Versals are best done at a 30° pen angle. There is a slight slant to the letters. The ideal height of these letters is 8 pen widths. Stem strokes are flared at top and bottom.

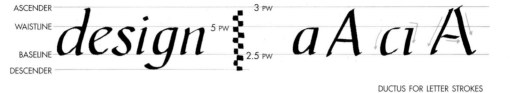

ASCENDER
WAISTLINE
BASELINE
DESCENDER

3 PW
design 5 PW
2.5 PW

aA a A

DUCTUS FOR LETTER STROKES

©2000 Lisa Engelbrecht

Castellar™

Castellar is a computer-generated typeface imitating carved letters found on an old Roman column. It has a refined look due to its incised appearance, with elegant variance in line weights in both the thick and thin strokes. It is a wonderful face to use on herb pots, as roman numerals on painted wall friezes, or on clocks, such as on page 92.

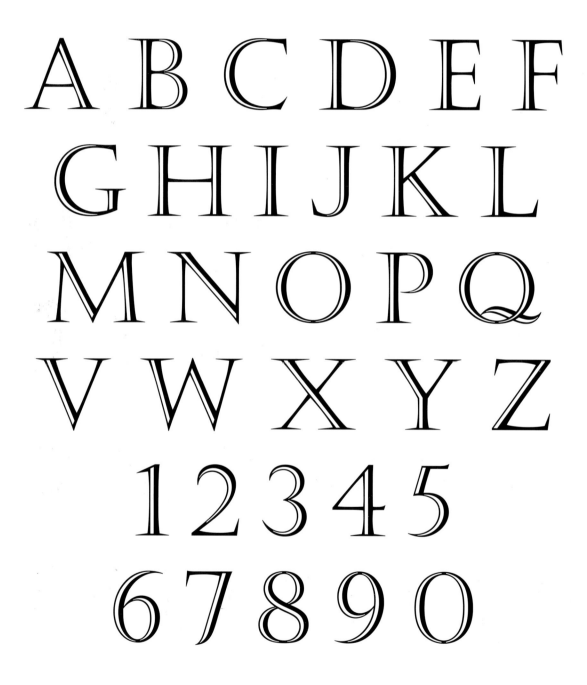

© Adobe Systems, Incorporated

Uncials

Uncials are normally a calligraphic hand created with a broad-tip pen, but this alphabet is presented instead for outline and filling. Adopted primarily for Christian text in the fourth through eighth centuries, Uncials preceded the development of lowercase letters (miniscules). Its chunky, Celtic appearance adds distinction to crafts and lends itself to widely spaced presentations, such as on page 100. Uncials have quite a bit of personality and are perfect for use in scrapbooks, notecards, scarves, and decorative plaques.

A b c d e F

G h i j k l m

n o p q r s t

u v w x y z

1 2 3 4 5 6 7 8 9

© 1999 Laura Donnelly Bethmann

Adobe Caslon

Caslon is the epitome of movable roman type. Its impressive history includes use in the first printings of the Declaration of Independence and the United States Constitution! This computer-generated version is versatile for tracing and filling in craft applications. Combine it with shadows for a decorative look (page 82) or chemically rust-painted letters for a vintage feel (page 94).

ABCDFGHI
JKLMNOPQ
RSVWXYZ
abcdfghijklm
nopqrstvwxyz
1234567890

© Adobe Systems Incorporated

Galliard Italic

This computer-generated version of an old-style typeface in its italic form has a distinctive presence appropriate for use with any craft project. The curved and angled letterforms may be more difficult to trace than other selections, but the result will be well worth the effort. Try these letters on memory boxes, vases, invitations, and pillows.

ABCDFGHI
JKLMNOPQ
RSVWXYZ

abcdfghijklm
nopqrstvwxyz
1234567890

©1998 International Typeface Corporation

"There's Time!" Kitchen Clock

"There's time! There's no hurry!" shouts this kitchen clock in Italian (and of course, in Italy, there's never a rush). This incised lettering was inspired by carved letters from an ancient Roman column and offers a refined counterpoint to the playful text. Placing text on a circle requires attention to detail but can be easily mastered. This technique for decorating glazed ceramics utilizes a craft marker and fixative instead of paint and brush, which may be easier for beginning lettering artists.

For this project you will need:

- white ceramic dinner plate with wide rim
- access to a ceramic drill (Have the hole for the clock works drilled into the plate before decorating the clock face. Trust me.)
- permanent, waterproof fine-point craft pen suitable for inking on glazed ceramics (Grumbacher makes a suitable pen)
- Castellar lettering guide
- graphite tracing paper
- fine rolling ball pen
- spray
- permanent fixative
- compass
- clock works
- clock hands
- craft knife

Lettering Technique

Placing text on a circle is as simple as imagining radiant lines exploding from the center of the circle—the vertical middle of each letter will follow these lines.

1.

2.

3.

4.

1. Because you won't be inking the letters from traced outlines, it's important to become familiar with the characteristics of the typeface. With a compass, draw a circle slightly larger than the inside diameter of the dinner plate rim on tracing paper. Enlarge the Castellar letters on a photocopier to the appropriate size to fit your plate. Trace the letters onto the compass-drawn baseline. The letters should point outward from the baseline following lines radiating from the center of the circle. Notice the subtleties of the letters, such as the thick to thin variations in the fine strokes of the letters.

2. Draw another circle with a compass on tracing paper, this time the diameter of the original circle plus the height of the capital letters. This will be the baseline of the capitals that point into the center and are placed at the bottom of the dinner plate. Trace the letters onto the compass-drawn baseline. The letters should point inward from the baseline following lines radiating from the center of the circle.

3. Take a good look at how the letters sit on each baseline. Because they were originally created to sit on a straight line, wider letters (such as M) do not follow a curve and will look as if they are straddling the circle. It's easy to correct this by extending the outside legs of the M to meet the baseline and adjusting the serif feet to follow the curve.

4. Unfortunately, graphite tracing paper leaves a residue that interferes with the use of the craft pen. Therefore, you should transfer only small dots at each join or along each curve to use as a connect-the-dots guide. After the dots are placed, use the craft pen to outline the letters, checking your traced guide often for reference. Fill in the thick lines as you go, being careful to not set your hand on the wet ink while lettering. When dry, make small corrections to the letterforms by carefully scraping with a craft knife. When finished, spray with permanent fixative according to manufacturer's directions.

ABCD **Variation** To add more color to these multiweight letters, outline the heavier leg with black and fill in the center with red or any other color that works well with your decor. You could also gild the inside of the letter (see page 34 for information on gilding).

Vintage Sap Bucket

Sap buckets are not only a staple in the maple syrup industry but also have become a popular home decorating accent. Recycled buckets are usually painted with a wash of color, which is helpful to syrup producers when searching for the buckets in the early morning mist! Lettering with wide spacing and a technique for creating real rusted type creates a historical appearance also appropriate for watering cans, mailboxes, and French flower buckets.

For this project you will need:

painted metal sap bucket

Caslon lettering guide

instant rust kit consisting of one container of ground iron in a water-based medium and one container of chemical rust finishing solution (a popular manufacturer is Modern Options)

small chisel-edged brush

very small round brush

disposable small round brush

tracing paper

pencil

graphite transfer paper

fine-point rolling ball pen

Lettering Technique

A chemical faux-finishing technique and wide letter spacing give an aged appearance to lettering.

Maple Maple

1.

Maple

2.

Maple

3.

Maple

4.

1. Wide letter spacing helps give this project a vintage look similar to Colonial American signage. Enlarge the Caslon lettering guide to your desired size, then trace the words "Pure Maple Syrup" with a pencil on tracing paper. Normal letter spacing would be like the example on the left, but for this project, you should extend the letter spacing (right).

2. Transfer the lettering to the sap bucket with graphite tracing paper and a fine, pointed pen. Begin filling in the outlines with the instant iron compound contained in the instant rust kit. This fluid consists of ground iron in a water-based medium; it works much like acrylic paint. Use a chisel-edged brush that is the same width as the widest strokes of the letters and adjust the angle of your brush as needed for smooth, simple strokes. Fill in details with a very small round brush, if necessary.

3. Continue filling in all the letterforms. It's not important that the edges be perfect—variances in the edges will add to the aged look of the finished piece. When you've filled in all the letters, let the base coat dry completely. Apply a second coat and let the piece cure for 24 hours.

4. Pour a small amount of the instant rust compound into a disposable container. Apply it to the cured lettering with a small pointed brush. Try to keep within the painted letterforms, as the compound will oxidize and create rust wherever it is applied. Don't worry if a small amount of the rust compound extends past the letters, though, because it will accentuate the handmade appearance of the letters. Let the lettering cure for at least two hours. Check the color of the rust and apply more rust compound if a deeper color is desired. Carefully dispose of all brushes used with the rust compound.

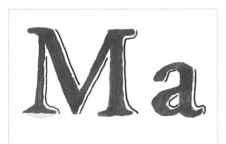

ABCD **Variation** Rust-creating chemicals don't appeal to everyone; luckily, many manufacturers of craft acrylics make special paints that adhere to metal surfaces like this sap bucket. Try using a metallic bronze paint to mimic the rust finish. Add a thin black rule with a fine liner brush on the right side of each letter stroke.

Four Seasons Placemats

Historical and romantic at the same time, letter rubbings of chiseled text have been an art form for centuries. Create them yourself by cutting out letters from cardboard, placing rice paper on top, and rubbing across the paper with pastels. For this project, completed rubbings were combined with color photocopies on clear acetate of seasonal botanicals that were placed directly on the photocopier bed. The collage was then color photocopied onto color heat transfer paper and ironed onto a set of placemats. Try incorporating your letter rubbings into collages, calendars, journals, and greeting cards.

For this project you will need:

- two-ply chipboard (lightweight cardboard)
- semihard or soft pastels in desired colors
- roman capital alphabet
- transfer paper
- pen
- craft knife
- bristol board
- straight-edge
- PVA glue
- rice paper or other soft, translucent paper
- color transfer paper for color copiers and ink-jet printers
- finely woven placemats or fabric
- coordinating ribbon
- fabric glue
- iron

Lettering Technique

Rubbing charcoal on tracing paper across the relief created by cardboard cut-out letters results in shadow like outlines.

1.

1. Enlarge your selected roman lettering guide to the desired size. Transfer the outlines of all the letters for each word onto lightweight cardboard. Because you'll assemble the words from the letters you cut out, it is not necessary to transfer the letters to the cardboard in any special order. Cut out each letterform from the cardboard with a craft knife. Turn the cardboard as you're cutting so that you're always trimming the cardboard in a direction that is comfortable to you. Correct any transferring mistakes with the craft knife.

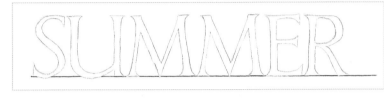

2.

2. When all of the letters have been cut out, assemble them into words on a piece of bristol board. Start by establishing the baseline with a straight-edge and a pencil. Glue each letter into its correct place on the baseline using PVA glue. Note the letters' positions on the baseline—the serifed feet of each letter will sit rght on the baseline, but the rounded beses of the *S* and *U* sit slightly below the baseline, as does the middle *v*-shape of the capital *M*.

3.

3. Place a piece of rice paper over the letters and begin rubbing with a piece of colored pastel or charcoal. The pastel color will collect on the edges and top of the letterforms, and the word will begin appearing on the paper, almost magically. Rub in a consistent diagonal direction for a stylish look, or rub in a circular motion for a more solid appearance. If the rubbing is going to be used as final art, a spray fixative to preserve the pastels.

Variation Instead of using the raised cardboard letterforms to create the rubbing (right), try using the cardboard that the letters were cut from to create a gravestonelike incised rubbing (left). The words should be cut from one piece of cardboard so no awkward spaces between words or letters show in the final rubbing, and all of the counters (spaces inside letterforms) must be glued back in place inside the cut-out letter openings.

Initial Painted Curtains

Customize your curtains in a sophisticated style by lettering them with Versals, a classical and historic form of capital letters traditionally used to begin verses. Choose the first initials of each family member's name, as Lisa has here, or use the whole alphabet for a playful addition to a child's room. This project utilizes acrylic ink instead of thicker fabric paint, though fabric paint would work well applied to thin fabrics with a flat brush. These semiformal letters become playful when placed at varying angles inside a strict placement grid. You could also initial pillows, table runners, book bags, and scarves.

For this project you will need:

purchased sheer curtains, or sew curtains in your selected fabric (natural fabric, such as 100% cotton, is recommended)

Versals lettering guide

air-soluble fabric marker

pearlescent acrylic ink

small pointed brush

Lettering Techniques

Formal Versals are made charming and whimsical by a sophisticated color palette and playful placement.

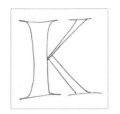

1.

1. Wash the curtains to remove any sizing. Using an air-soluble marker, outline your chosen letters on to the curtains, referring to the Versals lettering guide (exemplar). These marks will disappear in two or three days, so don't worry about making mistakes. If you decide to letter on to a synthetic fabric curtain, test the marker first on a hidden spot to confirm that the marker lines will disappear. For a playful appearance, tilt the letters randomly on the curtain. Follow the fabric's weave pattern, if appropriate, to help plan where the initials should fall, or create a template grid from brown kraft paper or tissue paper. If the curtain fabric is sheer enough, you can enlarge the Versal initials on page 84 and place the photocopies under the fabric as a see-through guide.

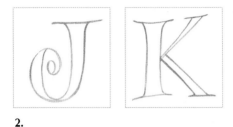

2.

2. Carefully outline each letter with a small pointed brush and pearlescent acrylic ink, following the final drawn outlines of your letter. You may find that you need to use more pressure with the brush when writing on fabric than when writing on paper, and your strokes may have to be retraced to create a solid fill. Reshape your brush often while painting to ensure a clean, sharp line on the fabric.

3.

3. With the same small pointed brush, flood the inside of the outline with the pearlescent ink. You may dilute the ink with a bit of water for ease of use, but be careful not to add too much, which may cause the ink to bleed in the fabric. Repeat all steps for each desired letter. Let dry completely. If you chose to use fabric paint rather than acrylic ink, heat set the paint according to manufacturer's recommendations.

4.

 **Variation** You can also create monograms on your curtains. Enlarge the initial of your family name for the large center letter and place it between your first and middle initial. Use white fabric paint on sheer white curtains for a sophisticated and subtle appearance. Carefully measure each monogram's placement, by making a template.

Vintage *Botanical Note Cards*

Uncials are a classic calligraphy hand, but here, Laura Bethmann has traced and filled the letterforms, a great way to learn the shapes of the individual letters before creating them traditionally with a calligraphy pen. Laura, the author of *Nature Printing with Herbs, Fruits and Flowers*, incorporates nature printing in the note cards, carefully mixing ink to the desired colors before printing with real botanicals. The delicate shading that colored pencils add to the letters complements the delicate patterns the leaves make when pressed onto the craft surface. You can decorate the envelopes as well to coordinate with the note cards.

For this project you will need:

blank note cards,
or watercolor paper folded
into a card shape

Uncial lettering guide

tracing paper

graphite pencil

colored pencils in green,
orange, and yellow

pencil sharpener

selected botanicals

water-based printing inks,
or other media such as acrylic
paints, stamp pads, or fabric
paints for the nature printing

sponge

tweezers

spray fixative if desired

Lettering Technique

*Calligraphic letterforms traced
and filled with colored pencil are
an easy way to add sophisticated
lettering to a project.*

100

1.

2.

3.

1. Enlarge the Uncial lettering guide to your desired size. Trace "autumn" in pencil on tracing paper. Notice how the U tucks in under the Crossbar of the T. Uncials are a very old letterform created before minuscules (lowercase letters) were developed. Use these letters in two sizes to simulate majuscules (uppercase letters) and minuscules. Rub the back of the tracing paper with the side of your pencil tip to make lead transfer paper. Place the tracing paper over your note card or watercolor paper and retrace the letters with a sharpened pencil to lightly transfer them to the paper. Purchased graphite transfer paper would result in a transferred line too heavy for this project and is difficult to clean from paper surfaces.

2. Fill in the letterforms with orange colored pencil, fading into lighter, feathered sections where desired. Add yellow colored pencil highlights to these lighter orange sections.

3. Fill in the blank areas with green pencil, shading lightly over the yellow areas and more heavily at the solid ends. Make the edges and corners of the letters crisp by outlining with sharp colored pencils. Add botanical prints by applying printing inks to one side of a leaf or flower with a sponge. Place the leaf on your card with tweezers, and cover with a clean sheet of paper. Press the leaf to tranfer the image, and remove the leaf with tweezers. Spray the final card with fixative to seal.

A B C D **Variation** Watercolors are another coloring option for this technique. Here, "herbs" was traced in pencil and lightly colored with watercolor. The edges were defined with a finely pointed watercolor brush and darker watercolor paint. The widely spaced letters provide ample space to add botanical prints of small herbs.

Vintage
Sweet Dreams Pillows

Give vintage linens a personal touch by stenciling your best wishes for a good night's sleep on them in hand-drawn letters. Janet used two shades of dry stencil paint to create an interior highlight in the letters for a subtle, heirloom appearance that complements the lace and embroidery on the pillows. When placed on a shallow curve, the hand drawn letters mimic old sign lettering. Stenciling is a technique that can be applied to almost any surface—try painting walls, picture frames, lamp shades, and furniture.

For this project you will need:

- vintage linens
- tracing paper
- transfer paper
- pencil
- heavyweight laminating film
- oil-based dry stencil paint in two shades of blue (and other desired colors)
- small stencil brushes
- craft knife

Lettering Technique

Stenciled letters are emphasized with an interior highlight created by blending two shades of a color.

1.

2.

3.

4.

1. Sketch "Sweet" and "Dreams" on tracing paper until you're satisfied with the design. Place the letters on a modified curve, as Janet has, but don't worry about keeping the letters exactly even. Avoid closing the letterforms completely so the stencil can remain in one piece when cut. For example, the bars on the lowercase e's do not extend to the outside curve—if they did, the center counter of the letter would have to be replaced manually when stenciling.

2. When you're happy with the design, transfer the lettering to heavyweight laminating film, an adhesive-backed clear film that creates a tight seal between the stencil and the fabric, preventing paint creep on the final project. Cut out the stencil with a craft or stencil knife and place it on your fabric, carefully sealing the edges with your fingers. Fill in the letters with light blue dry stencil paint and a small stencil brush, using smooth brushing motions.

3. Create the interior highlight by applying darker blue dry stencil paint at the top and bottom of each letter, leaving the inside the lighter blue shade that was already applied. The dry stencil paint takes a long time to dry, so the two colors will blend easily. Use a light, lifting stroke when creating the gradient. Test the effect on scrap fabric first to gain experience making the strokes necessary to create the gradient between shades.

4. Add stenciled embellishments to the lettering as desired.

A B C D **Variation** Once you perfect your paint blending technique, you can blend any colors to fill stenciled letters. Brushstrokes can either be strong, to add texture, or light, for a smooth fill. Add these decorative letters to any wood or fabric project.

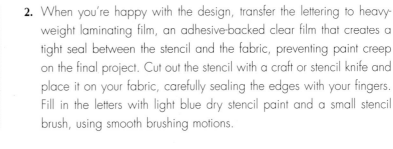

Hot Pepper Oil Bottle

Homemade flavored olive oil becomes a perfect housewarming gift when the glass container is hand painted with this vibrant vintage lettering. Yellow-orange flames emphasize the heat of the oil, and the pointed ornaments on the type add an old-style, decorative element to the letterforms. Use your color palette to convey context on the labels—red and orange are perfect for hot pepper oil, greens for rosemary-flavored oil, and light tans and gold for garlic-flavored oil. This lettering would also be perfect for toyboxes, kitchen canisters, and frames.

For this project you will need:

flat-sided glass olive oil container

water-based oven-firing glass paints in brown, red, and light orange

Caslon or Bodoni lettering guide

tracing paper

graphite transfer paper

pen

small round or spotting natural-hair brush

very small liner brush

Lettering Technique

Adding accents and special fills to letterforms creates a vintage appearance for decorative applications.

1.

1. Enlarge the lettering guide as needed. Draw a baseline on tracing paper and trace all capital letters onto the baseline. Draw another horizontal line midway through the letters and extend small triangle ornaments to each side of the letter, as shown.

2.

2. Transfer the outlines of the ornamented type to the glass surface with graphite transfer paper and a pen. With a very small round or spotting brush, begin outlining the letters with the brown paint. Work slowly and carefully, and be careful where you rest your hand—you don't want to wipe away any of the transfer lines by mistake! Let the paint dry completely when finished, then carefully clean up mistakes by lightly scraping with a craft knife or straight-edge razor.

3.

3. Fill the inside of each letter with red paint and a small round brush. The first coat of paint may not have the even coverage you want and may also shrink a bit while drying, so let dry and apply a second coat, slightly overlapping the brown outlines. Let dry completely.

4.

4. Add pointed accents inside the letters with the very small round brush and orange paint. Paint curves at the midpoint of rounded letter strokes and paint triangles at the top and bottom of straight letter strokes. Apply a second coat if accents are not strong enough after one application. Let dry, then oven fire according to paint manufacturer's directions.

A B C D **Variation** Red and orange are perfect colors for hot pepper-flavored oil, but try moss green and metallic gold for rosemary or other herb-flavored oils. A black outline will strongly define the letters against the glass bottle.

Hand-Lettered Crafts
GALLERY

P ersonalizing homemade crafts by adding hand lettering can be explored in many artistic media. The following gallery showcases crafts that take lettering one step further: lettering as wall decoration, on floor cloths, quilts, and spice jars, and as a collaborative process among a group of friends for creating a yearlong calendar. Also featured are techniques such as exquisite dyed silk, wood carving, acrylic gel transfer, and metal and glass etching. Brush lettering becomes fine art on lamp shades and decoupaged plates. Lettering moves into the third dimension when you cut letters from craft foam and cover them in moss to create a movable display. There's no limit to the inspiration you can take from these artists!

Moss-Covered Letters

Ingrid Nowak

Ingrid Nowak created these charming and simple letters with sheet moss and foam core. She simply transferred lightweight sans-serif letterforms to a sheet of foam core, carefully cut them out, and applied clumps of green sheet moss to each letter with spray adhesive. Ingrid prefers her letters simple and unadorned but notes that crafters could also wrap them with raffia ribbon for more decorative effects to coordinate with a room's decor or holiday theme.

Decorative Lettering in the Home

Charlene "Charley" Ayuso Cooper and Rene Genung

Decorative artist Charlene "Charley" Ayuso Cooper teamed up with lettering artist Irene Genung to create this beautiful and personal room for Charlene's daughter, Gabriela Sophia. After Charley finished the walls in an eighteenth-century European glazing style with *trompe l'oeil* starfish, a Pompeii Wave wall frieze, and ribbon banner, Irene stepped in to add the lettering. She worked on paper with charcoal first to plan the layout of the quotations. She created a pounce pattern following the final design with a pounce wheel, taped the paper to the wall, and dusted the pattern with charcoal dust or talc to transfer the outlines. She then painted the letters using lacquer-based metallic gold paint and flat and quill brushes. When the paint dried, she used a chamois cloth to remove all traces of the charcoal and talc lettering guides.

Spice Jars

Lisa Holtzman

Lisa has a quirky lettering style all her own, and these spice jars are just the right vehicle for their playful and fun application. She first sketched the lettering on tracing paper. When she was satisfied with each design, she inserted the lettering sketch inside the jar against the clear glass wall to use as a template for painting on the outside. She used black water-based cloisonné outliner that is heat set in the oven to create the dimensional lettering by painting directly from the tube. She applied semi-opaque paints that are also heat set to create small icons of the spice on each bottle.

Lettered Silk Scarf

Lynn M. Slevinsky

Canadian calligrapher Lynn Slevinsky lettered this silk scarf in compressed italic—the same hand she used when lettering certificates presented during the 1998 Winter Olympics in Calgary. She wrote the letters with a large brass pen, then placed them under the scarf as a template. The outlines of the letters were traced with a permanent, colored resist, then filled in with Procion H dyes, which she also used to paint the background of the scarf. In addition to her calligraphy artwork, Lynn is the author of *Marker Lettering*, volumes 1, 2, and 3.

Watermelon Decoupage Plate

Judy Kastin

This acclaimed example of fine lettering was created by author and calligrapher Judy Kastin. She used a black Pentel color brush to write the pointed brush lettering (a Mark Twain quotation) and to create the watermelon seeds, adding highlights and shadows with assorted gel pens afterward. First, the lettering was completed on red rice paper, hand-torn with a feathered edge into a circle slightly larger than the center section of the plate. The paper was then decoupaged to the back of the glass plate, combined with a collage of hand-torn sheets of green rice paper that overlapped the outer edge of the red circle and each other on the plate rim. Decoupage glue was not applied to the center area of the plate; it was used only on the underside of the glass rim and then the back of just the green papers to seal.

Brush-Lettered Lamp Shades

Eliza S. Holliday

Brush lettering becomes fine art in these lamp shades designed by Eliza Holliday, co-author of the instructional brush calligraphy book *Brush Lettering*. Eliza letters purchased lamp shades with gouache and a pointed Oriental brush. The pointed brush is flexible enough to let her write lightly with the tip or to bear down heavily for bolder words. Gouache is a flexible medium that can be mixed to various textures and shades of color depending on the amount of water added. The result is a visual treat where quotations become layers of dark and light and are graphically beautiful, whether you take the time to read them or not. Once the paint dries, the lamp shades are sprayed with a fixative or varnish to prevent smudging.

Tempus Fugit

Mary W. Hart

Mary Hart, a fine artist and professional calligrapher, created this clock from a purchased unfinished cabinet. A whimsical combination of Italic, Modern Roman, and pointed pen lettering adorns the cabinet inside and out. The phrases were created with acrylic paint and washes utilizing both a pen and a small brush appropriate to the particular lettering style. The small drawer at the bottom holds loose feathers—a perfect symbol of time flying!

Dreaming Kitty

JoAnne Powell

Professionally taught calligrapher JoAnne Powell began incorporating lettering into her quilting in 1986 when her son came home from kindergarten reciting a poem about leprechauns. She decided to save the moment in a quilt. "What was I thinking?" she says, "I couldn't have just recorded the poem with a video camera?" Thus began many years of widely exhibited, award-winning lettered quilting. "Dreaming Kitty" features fish names in New World Neuland hand, created with acrylic paint and a synthetic flat brush applied to the fabric after cutting but before sewing.

Brushed Gold Vase

Judy Kastin

Here's a beautiful way to create a metallic gold finish on glass without gilding. Judy Kastin, author of *100 Keys to Great Calligraphy* and co-author of the *Speedball Textbook*, created this sophisticated and classic vase by writing pointed brush letters with a brown Pentel color brush onto pieces of gold tissue paper, which were then decoupaged to the inside surface of the glass with decoupage glue. More decoupage glue was then applied to the back sides of the papers to seal them. She drew stars on the outside of the glass with a silver pointed metallic marker and applied gold metallic wax to the upper lip of the vase. When the glue was dry, the wax was also applied to the inside tissue for additional highlights.

Gocco-Printed Calendar Pages

PEN IN HAND COLLABORATIVE: Joan B. Machinchick, Jan Lynn, Lynne Carnes, Suzanne Heany, Marilyn Gaver, and Tamara Stoneburner

Born from a small group of friends who enjoy both lettering and crafts, the Pen in Hand Collaborative has been creating calendars for many years. Each member creates two calendar pages based on a chosen theme such as the Middle Ages. Each page is then gocco-printed in quantity on fine art paper. Not only does the collaborative make enough to share but they also sell the calendars successfully at craft shows. Each member designs her pages to reflect her individual style; the chosen theme, consistent page size, paper, and printing technique unify the pages.

Tea Tray Floor Cloth

Laurie Zallen, *Poppy Yoyo*

This fabulous floor cloth incorporating a Lewis Carroll quotation from the Mad Hatter's tea party in *Alice in Wonderland* is a wonderful example of stylish and whimsical lettering. Laurie begins making a floor cloth by stretching heavy canvas and treating it with gesso. She then applies coats and coats of acrylic paint to complete her desired pattern and finishes the cloth with many layers of water-based varnish. She first sketched this dynamic lettering lightly in pencil to plan the design. Then she painted the letters with black acrylic paint and a pointed brush. A special note: Laurie's floor cloth production is a family affair, as her father, "Poppy," assists in the cutting, sanding, drafting, and finishing of each floor cloth Laurie creates.

Mosaic "T" Tray

Sandra Salamony

This playful double-entendre tea tray is a study in shadows. Using only four shades of blue, distinctive letterforms were painted on ceramic tiles with oven firing enamel paint. Then a different style of shadow was added to each tile, including hard diagonal shadows, inside shadows emphasizing depth, and a whimsical stretched shadow at the foot of a leaning capital *T*.

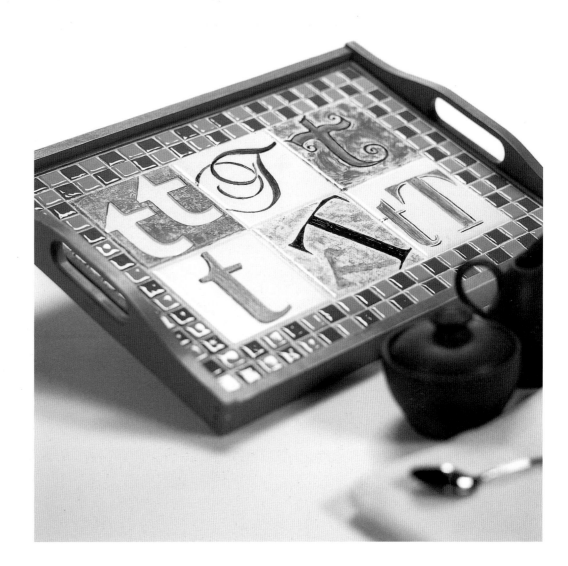

Celebrate! Plate

Judith Bain Dampier

Painting in reverse on the back of a plate may seem daunting, but lettering artist Judith Bain Dampier makes it look easy. She intends for her plates to be used, so she limits the painting surface to the back of a clear glass plate. She first designs her lettering on a sheet of clear plastic film that, when complete, is taped to the front of the plate. When the plate is turned over, the backward letters can be easily read through it. She used gloss oven-firing water-based paints to create these drawn Versals with a pointed brush and notes that you should allow each layer of paint to dry before adding another. Remember that the colors will appear in reverse order when the plate is turned forward, so careful planning is recommended.

Image Transfer Mosaic Mirror

Sandra Salamony

T his evocative mirror, made from tumbled marble tiles, was created with an image transfer process utilizing matte acrylic gel medium, a safe, water-based alternative to solvent-based transfer processes. The lettering was originally handwritten on white bristol board with a small pointed brush and calligraphy ink. It was digitally combined with scans of autumn leaves that had been placed directly on the scanner bed, which created dimensional shadows. A color laser printout was made of the final design. A layer of acrylic matte medium was wiped on the marble tiles with a foam brush. The color laser printout was then placed face-down on the tile and rubbed smooth with a brayer. After the gel completely dried (overnight), the paper was carefully soaked off the tile to reveal the reversed, transferred image.

Family Tribute Box

Paula Grasdal

Mixed media artist Paula Grasdal created this collage box as a tribute to her grand-father, beginning a projected collection of boxes that will become a visual family tree when hung together. She transferred old-style roman text to a piece of color-washed balsa wood with transfer paper and a stylus to create an outlined impression of the letters. Then, she carefully carved out the interior of the letters with a craft knife utilizing a small pointed blade, following the transfer lines. She painted the interiors of the letters with turquoise and metallic gold acrylic paint and a small pointed brush to add an aged verdegris effect that complements the collection of memorabilia.

Etched Metal Jewelry Box

Veronica E. Tucker, *Miz V. Designs*

A rtist Veronica Tucker uses permanent ink as a resist to create the dimensional lettering in her metalwork. The copperplate-inspired script letters and border are penned with a permanent marker on a copper sheet. The copper piece is then suspended in personal computer board etchant solution, an extremely caustic liquid used to etch computer motherboards. After the etching process is complete, cupric nitrate is applied, adding a patina to the surface of the copper. The patina is then painstakingly scraped from the letters' surface to reveal the original copper beneath.

Lettering Resources

Vintage and Computer-Generated Typefaces

Once you are interested in lettering arts, you'll never look at billboards in the same way again! Look at lettering everywhere for inspiration. Comics, signs, CD covers, and posters often feature lettering examples from traditional to cutting-edge typography. If you live near a college, take a good look at homemade flyers and posters for local bands and gallery shows—they often include experimental examples of design and typography.

For more traditional and vintage samples, start a collection of advertising prints and tins featuring manufacturer's logos. You can find these at antique shops. Also available at antique stores are many, many old books whose chapters often begin with special drop capitals, ornate letters that start a paragraph. If you're lucky, you might also find a printer's sample book of type, a wonderful resource for unusual and fun collections of alphabets.

Many of these vintage examples are conveniently collected into books of copyright-free art, also known as clip art. The best-known collections are published by Dover Publications, though other companies compile similar books. These collections can be found featuring typographic samples and alphabets in styles ranging from Renaissance to art deco and art nouveau. Often, alphabets featured in these collections are incomplete, but they are usually inspiring nonetheless.

For more examples of trace-and-fill lettering, search through stencil companies' selections and needlework templates. You'll also find many books that feature lettering on paper techniques for scrapbooking fans.

Of course, many, many computer typefaces are available. The International Typeface Company and Adobe are two of the best known and most trusted companies in this arena. See their Websites at www.itcfonts.com and www.adobe.com respectively.

Calligraphy

If the calligraphy section of this book inspires you to learn more, check your local adult education organization for evening classes—calligraphy is a popular subject in many localities. Also inquire at local colleges for their extension school listings, as many offer coursework in the lettering arts.

Local, national, and international calligraphy guilds are a wonderful resource for book recommendations and workshops and for finding a supportive community of lettering artists. Begin by checking with the Association for the Calligraphic Arts, which lists member guilds throughout the United States, Canada, Japan, China, and other international locations.

Association for the Calligraphic Arts (ACA)

> 1100-H Brandywine Boulevard
> P.O. Box 3388
> Zanesville, OH 43702-3388
> (740) 452-4541
> aca@calligraphicarts.org
> www.calligraphicarts.org

Two great resources for calligraphic publications and supplies are:

Paper and Ink Books
P.O. Box 35
3 N. Second Street
Woodsboro, MD 21798
(301) 898-7991
(800) PEN-7772
paperinkbk@aol.com
www.paperinkbooks.com

John Neal Bookseller
1833 Spring Garden Street
Greensboro, NC 27403
(336) 272-6139
(800) 369-9598 (USA and Canada)
info@JohnNealBooks.com
www.johnnealbooks.com/

If you have access to the Internet, you'll find many downloadable calligraphy instruction pages (as well as a catalog of lettering supplies) in .pdf format from Speedball:

Speedball Art Products
P.O. Box 5157
Statesville, NC 28687
www.speedballart.com

Finally, here are two periodicals that will inspire you with their instruction and lettering examples:

Somerset Studio
22992 Mill Creek, Suite B
Laguna Hills, CA 92653
(949) 380-7318
www.somersetstudio.com

Letter Arts Review
P.O. Box 9986
Greensboro, NC 27429
(336) 272-6139
(800) 348-PENS (USA and Canada)
www.johnnealbooks.com/lar/

Many of the contributors to this book are authors of lettering instruction books, all of which are highly recommended:

100 Keys to Great Calligraphy, by Judy Kastin
North Light Books

Brush Lettering, by Marilyn Reaves
  and Eliza Schulte
Design Books
The Lyons Press

Marker Lettering, volumes 1, 2 and 3, by Lynn Slevinsky
Summer Magic Books
38 Strathroy Bay S.W.
Calgary, AB, Canada T3H 1J9
http://members.home.com/summermagic

The Speedball Textbook: A Comprehensive Guide to Pen and Brush Lettering, edited by Joanne Fink and Judy Kastin

Speedball Art Products Company

Directory of Artists

Laura Donnelly Bethmann
Laura Bethmann Studios
110 Locust Street
Tuckerton, NJ 08087
(609) 296-7219
laurastudio@pro-usa.net

Gina M. Brown
4590 Bartlett Road
Williamsburg, MI 49690
gmsbrown@aol.com

Isabel Lynne Carnes
508 Mystic Lane
Arnold, MD 21012
(410) 757-0548
gpcarnes@aol.com

Charlene "Charley" Ayuso Cooper
Faux Finish Studio, Inc.
2100 San Ramon Valley Boulevard, Suite 6
San Ramon, CA 94583
(925) 362-4510
fauxceo@aol.com

Judith Bain Dampier
921 90th Avenue
Dawson Creek, BC
Canada V1G1A3
(250) 782-1316
judith@pris.bc.ca

Lisa Engelbrecht
Lisa Engelbrecht Design
6329 Mariquita Street
Long Beach, CA 90803
(562) 598-5168
lengelbrecht@earthlink.net

Marilyn L. Gaver
413 Fernwood Drive
Severna Park, MD 21146
(410) 315-8434
music@toad.net

Rene Genung
Artistry by Rene
20885 Redwood Road #140
Castro Valley, CA 94541
(510) 481-8191
realfaux@aol.com

Paula Grasdal
437 Trapelo Rd.
Belmont, MA 02478
(617) 489-4717
pgrasdal@netway.com

Mary W. Hart
251 Forest St.
Winchester, MA 01890
(781) 729-3306
hart251@msn.com

Suzanne M. Heany
484 Ixworth Court
Severna Park, MD 21146
(410) 647-8339

Eliza S. Holliday
Eliza Lettering Design
129 S. 17th Street
Fernandina Beach, FL 32034
(904) 277-4834
eliza@cains.com

Lisa Holtzman
1809 Oak Street, Apt. B
Santa Monica, CA 90405
(310) 450-6488

Judy Kastin
603 Bond Court
Merrick, NY 11566
(516) 292-8539
jkastin1@aol.com

Margaret Lammerts
Box 127
Tofield, AB
Canada T0B4J0
(780) 662-3061
lammarg@telusplanet.net

Jane W. Lynn
305 Riggs Avenue
Severna Park, MD 21146
(410) 647-3727

Joan B. Machinchick
Lake Claire Design Studio
P.O. Box 9792
Arnold, MD 21012
(410) 974-0139
lakeclaire@toad.net

Joan L. Merrell
2312 Allison Drive
Jefferson City, MO 65109
(573) 635-5116
joanmerrell@juno.com

Ingrid Nowak
(617) 725-6043
nowdel@aol.com

Janet Pensiero
263 Dupont Street
Philadelphia, PA 19128
(215) 487-2553
janetpensiero@gateway.net

JoAnne Powell
P.O. Box 433
Bellport, NY 11713-0433

Cindy Romo
712 4th Street East
Saskatoon, SK
Canada S7H1K2
(306) 665-7892

Sandra Salamony
80 Chestnut Street #4
Cambridge, MA 02139
(617) 491-7623
sandranoel@aol.com

Lynn M. Slevinsky
Summer Magic Books
38 Strathroy Bay SW
Calgary, AB
Canada T3H1J9
(403) 242-8561
summermagic@home.com

Tamara M. Stoneburner
Gracestone Calligraphics
20683 Pomeroy Court
Ashburn, VA 20147
(703) 858-0987
tms@gracestone.com

Veronica E. Tucker
Miz V. Designs
4 Lantern Lane
Georgetown, MA 01833
(978) 352-7809
vetucker@yahoo.com

Laurie Zallen
Poppy Yoyo
71 Wiswall Road
Newton, MA 02459
(617) 965-2433

About the Author

Sandra Salamony is an award-winning art director and writer in Cambridge, Massachusetts. She is co-author, with Mary Ann Hall, of *The Crafter's Project Book*, published by Rockport Publishers. Her craft designs have been featured in *Country Living's Handmade Frames*, and in many other books and magazines.